PARTiES
WITH A PURPOSE

KAROL LADD

THOMAS NELSON PUBLISHERS
Nashville, Tennessee

Published in Nashville, Tennessee, by Thomas Nelson Publishers,
Inc.

Scripture quotations are from the NEW KING JAMES VERSION
of the Bible. Copyright © 1979, 1980, 1982, Thomas Nelson,
Inc., Publishers.

Library of Congress Cataloging-in-Publication Data

Ladd, Karol.
    Parties with a purpose / Karol Ladd.
      p.   cm.
    ISBN 0-8407-4043-3
  1. Children's parties. 2. Games. 3. Activity programs in
Christian education. I. Title.
GV1205.L33 1993
793.2′1—dc20
                                             93-6036
                                              CIP

Printed in the United States of America

3 4 5 6 7 – 98 97 96

Acknowledgments

I want to give a big round of applause to all of the wonderful kids who participated in these parties!

Many thanks to Connie and Beth Dykhuizen, Holly Roman, and Lisa Schubert for their time and encouragement with this book. Special thanks to my friends Carol, Holly, Brenda, Janet, Amy, Leslie, Katy, Linda, and Tracy who helped me have a little more time to write.

I am truly grateful to my dad, Garry Kinder, who has motivated and inspired me throughout the years.

Most of all, I want to thank my precious family: Curt, Grace and Joy, for their understanding, love, and help during my work on this project.

Contents

Introduction

Creative parties make marvelous memories. While there are some people who feel a sense of excitement and anticipation in planning a party, most of us tend to feel anxious or inadequate, especially when planning a party for children. Relax. *Parties with a Purpose* has simple, imaginative, budget-minded ideas to help even the most uncreative party-givers make lasting memories for their children.

This party book is unique because it offers party themes that emphasize biblical values. Your guests will go home with more than just party favors; they will be taking with them a lesson from God's Word.

Parties with a Purpose is not just for birthday parties. You can use the ideas in this book for family devotions, vacation Bible school, Sunday school, Wednesday night church activities, choir parties, and youth retreats. Every child can benefit from learning truths from the Bible, so make the most of every opportunity.

Parties with a Purpose has done the thinking for you. Just choose a party and follow the instructions provided. Before you begin, let me give you a few components that go into making a successful party.

The most important step in throwing a children's party is planning. The earlier you plan, the easier the party will be to give. Begin choosing a theme about two months before the party date. By planning early, you can avoid the last-minute rush. You will have the time to make creative invitations and decorations for the party. I know that your free time is limited, so I have tried to keep the time required to prepare for each party to a minimum. By planning ahead, you can spread the work out over a period of time, and it will seem like little or no effort at all.

In choosing a theme, ask for input from the expert in your house—your child. Offer four or five party suggestions and let the birthday child decide. As your child gets older, seeking his or her opinion is especially important. You do not want your son or daughter to be embarrassed by something that you thought was cute but in reality was unacceptable to peers.

Another question to consider is where to have the party. Although many people choose to have parties at other locations, my first choice is to have the party at home. Children and parents seem to feel very comfortable in a home. A home is personal and inviting. If you feel that you need more space, you may want to consider having the party at your church or at a local recreation center. Some places charge a small fee for their use; others require a deposit, which will be returned to you if you leave the place clean and undamaged. I have suggested alternate locations for several of the theme parties within the chapters.

Cost is another consideration when throwing a party. Most of the parties in this book are fairly inexpensive. The party budgets are flexible, so that you can spend as much or as little as you want. For example, the "Favors" section of each chapter offers a long list of theme-related party favors. Pick and choose from the list to fit your budget. You'll find it is possible to have fun parties at a small cost.

Parties with a Purpose is separated into three sections according to age groups: ages two to five, ages six to nine, and ages ten to fifteen. Each section begins with an overview which will offer helpful information about each age group.

I did not include first birthday parties. For your child's first birthday, have a special family celebration complete with gifts, grandparents, cake, and decorations. Take lots of pictures of this memorable, yet simple, celebration. Save the kinds of parties I describe here for when your child is truly old enough to enjoy them.

Invitations, greetings, and thank you notes are important aspects of any party. I have found that children love to receive homemade and personalized invitations. Fun theme invitations build excitement and anticipation for the party. Consider the suggestions I have given in this book, and remember that if you plan ahead, it won't take you long to make the invitations. As your child gets older, be sure to let him help make the invitations.

Decide how many children to invite to the party. I have suggested an appropriate size for each party. Make your decision based on the location of the party, the friendships involved, and your own sanity (how many children do you think you can handle?). In some cases it is hard to scale down the invitation list, so ask several friends to help you with a large party. Don't forget to let your spouse and your other children get into the action. Make the party a family event. If you are concerned that some of the guests or their parents would be offended by the biblical message, you may want to include a few words on the invitation about the values which will be taught. The parent may then decide whether the child will attend the party.

An initial warm greeting is an essential element in any party, yet few people realize its importance. A warm, kind greeting sets the tone for the party. Have someone stand at the door to meet each guest with a friendly smile. Sometimes arriving at a party can be a threatening experience, and a friendly greeter can make all the difference as to how your guests feel about being there.

Writing thank-you notes seems to be a dying practice. Don't let that be the case at your home. Encourage your child to write his own thank-you notes, even at an early age. If he can write only his name, have him sign each card. It is important to help your child form the habit of writing thank-you notes when he is young, so that it will come naturally when he is grown.

The suggested party foods are simple to prepare and enjoyable for the children. I did not choose elaborate recipes that require gourmet talents. In each chapter, you will find creative ways to serve normal, everyday food. Do not forget that ages two to five are more susceptible to choking than older children are. Be sure to cut up any foods that could become caught in their throats, such as hot dogs (cut lengthwise), grapes, and cheese chunks. Avoid popcorn and hard candies for the young ones too.

Opening presents is another exciting element of a birthday party. Children look forward to this part of the celebration, so do not skip it. Many times, opening presents can become chaotic, with everyone trying to see the birthday child open his gifts, so each party chapter contains ideas to keep the present-opening time organized and entertaining.

While your children are still young, invest in a Polaroid camera. The camera will bring loads of fun to every party. Your guests will love receiving a picture of the event to take home as a favor. You can even make creative theme-related frames for the pictures and to give as favors.

Always remember that these special events are for the children and not to impress other parents with your wealth or creative talents. The best reward you can receive is to have a group of smiling, happy children at the end of the party. I'll never forget the day of my three-year-old daughter's Bear Birthday Party. After all the guests had gone home, she turned to me with a big smile on her face and said, "Mommy, thank you for my Bear Birthday Party. I love you." She knew I had expressed my love for her by putting the effort into giving her a special party.

In these busy times, one of the easiest birthday party solutions seems to be to take all of the children to someplace like "Papa's Pizza Party House." Keep in mind that children can go there anytime. By putting a little extra time into throwing a party, you can give your child a gift from your heart and from the Bible (rather than from your pocketbook). A special party is a gift he will remember for a lifetime. Our children are worth the extra effort.

Happy partying!

Ages Two Through Five

Preschool children are cute, active, and totally unpredictable. One moment a toddler can be fun and full of smiles, and the next moment he might throw a temper tantrum. Toddlers' entertainment and happiness come from simple pleasures, not from elaborate and expensive endeavors. Do not worry about impressing them with parties of grandeur. Toddlers love simply playing together.

The preschool years cover a span of developmental stages. Therefore, it's important to know how younger preschoolers differ from older ones.

Two year olds love to explore and play. They have a tremendous curiosity that is coupled with frustration because they cannot do all that they want to do. If you are having a party attended mainly by two year olds, ask their mothers to stay at the party to help with them. Each mother can help her child through games and crafts, and she can handle any tantrums that her child throws. Also, limit the number of two year olds that you invite. Six to eight two year olds is a nice number. If you invite more than ten, be prepared for some chaos and plan mainly large group activities like singing and games.

These little ones may be overwhelmed as they enter a party, so greet them at the door with a gentle hug and give them time to warm up to the new environment. They may not want to participate immediately in party activities. That's OK. They will feel comfortable after a while. With this age group you will also want to keep the games and crafts very simple. Be aware that some of the children may not want to participate. Keep as many children interested as possible, but do not worry about one or two stragglers. Let them do their own thing; they will probably join the group when they see how much fun the other children are having.

Three and four year olds are much easier to handle. They are generally more independent, adaptive, and cooperative than two year olds. Communication is easier; you can tell these children what you want and they can tell you what they want. They are able to participate more fully in games and crafts. Some three and four year olds still need time to warm up to the party environment, so be patient as they arrive.

At this age, children ask many questions. Try to satisfy their curiosity with a brief answer. If you do not know the answer, remind them that there are some questions that only God can answer. Three and four year olds love to run around and use a lot of their abundant energy, so the parties include many action games. They are also old enough to sit and listen to a story. Visual aids are a necessity, however. They need something to look at to help them understand and to keep their interest as you talk.

Parents of three and four year olds can stay or leave depending on how independent their children are. Invite between eight and ten three and four year olds to your party. You can probably handle a few more if you have help from other adults.

At age five, several transitions are taking place. Five year olds are beginning to grow out of preschool attitudes and actions and beginning to feel a little more grown up and independent. Some of your guests may have already started kindergarten. They are starting to form friendships and learning to display manners and to show respect. They listen fairly well and can be good helpers. At age five, children enjoy participating in most games, and they listen well to stories. Between eight to twelve guests is a nice number, but up to fifteen guests should not be too difficult if you have other adult help. The children's parents do not need to stay; in fact, sometimes it is best if they do not. But welcome parents who choose to stay and provide some snacks for them.

Preschool parties should last no more than an hour and a half— perhaps just an hour for two year olds. After all the excitement, children tend to get tired, and so do their parents, so it is best to keep the party short and end on a happy note.

Preschool parties usually include both boys and girls. You will probably want to choose a theme that fits your child's gender, even if you invite both boys and girls. For instance, the farm party may work better for a boy's party theme, but girls will still have a fantastic time at the party. The "Dandy Dolly" party is the only party that is just for girls, for obvious reasons.

Always be careful with balloons and other items that a small child might choke on. Sometimes younger siblings come to the parties, too, so keep the balloons out of reach (I use helium balloons for this purpose) and put small toys and candies out of reach. When a balloon breaks, pick up all of the balloon pieces immediately.

Preschool parties can be some of your child's earliest, happiest childhood memories. Take lots of pictures to keep the party memories forever. May you have a perfectly precious preschool party!

* 1 *

Noah's Ark Party

All aboard for a ride on Noah's ark! Guests will dress up as the animals on the ark and act out this marvelous story from Genesis. After the children play animal games and make a rainbow, they will enjoy animal sandwiches and a rainbow cake. The theme will come from Genesis chapters 7 through 9, the story of Noah trusting in God.

➡ **Suggested Size:**   5 to 12 children
    Suggested Time of Day: morning or afternoon
    Type: boys, girls, or both

YOU WILL NEED:

- Construction paper
- Geometric compass
- Glue
- Felt
- Poster boards
- Animal-shaped stickers
- Stuffed animals

- Large box
- Small plastic animals
- Animal crackers
- Balloons and crepe paper streamers
- Large hoop

INVITATIONS:

Make your invitations shaped like an ark with a door that opens to reveal the party information. Use brown poster board or construction paper to cut out simple ark shapes. Cut a door for each ark and fold it back. Glue white construction paper on the back of the invitation so that the information will show through the door. Write the information as you see below.

God told Noah to build an ark,
There was a lot of work, so he had to start.
We're glad that Noah chose to obey,
So let's celebrate on _____(child's name)_____ birthday!
The time is _____, and _____ is the date.
We'll all climb aboard the ark, so don't be late.
_____ is the address to note.

Dress as an animal that was on the boat.
We'll have a great time, just wait and see.
And don't forget to RSVP!
_____(phone number)_____

Place animal-shaped stickers on the ark and on the envelope. You can find stickers at card shops, Christian book stores, and craft stores.

DECORATIONS:

Gather all of the stuffed animals that you can find in your house and borrow some from your friends. You may want to look for some inexpensive inflatable animals as well. Place animals everywhere in the party room. You can put them on coffee tables, end tables, shelves, chairs, and couches. Your guests will want to play with them, so go ahead and let them. If there are any special animals that children should not handle, put them on high shelves where they can be seen but not touched.

Purchase balloons and streamers in rainbow colors. Hang the streamers from the tops of the doorways. Arrange the different colored strips to look like a rainbow. The children will color a giant rainbow banner as they arrive, and this banner can be used as a decoration once they have finished.

Make name tags to look like clouds with rainbows behind them. Use white construction paper to make the cloud and attach rainbow-colored ribbon to the back of each one. Pin the tags on the guests' clothing with safety pins.

At your front door or the entrance to the party room, place a small ark for the children to enter. This decoration will be used later for a game. To make the ark, get a large box from a store that sells appliances or furniture. Boxes for washing machines, dryers, large TVs, refrigerators, and some pieces of furniture are usually large enough. Open the box on both ends so that the children can walk or crawl through the box as they enter the party. Cut brown poster board (or white poster board painted brown) and staple or tape it to the sides of the box to look like the deck of the boat. To represent water around the ark, lay blue sheets or blue wrapping paper on the floor. For a ramp, take a 3-foot by 5-foot piece of plywood and nail a small block of wood to one end so that one side is elevated. Then the "animals" can walk up a slight incline to go into the ark.

For a centerpiece on the refreshment table make a smaller version of the ark using a shoe box covered with brown construction paper and plastic animals.

SCHEDULE: 1½ hours

15 minutes—Arrive, play, and color
15 minutes—Animal games
10 minutes—Story time
20 minutes—Lunch or snacks and cake
10 minutes—Rainbow craft
10 minutes—Open presents
10 minutes—Play time

ACTIVITIES:

1. Arrive, play, and color

As the children arrive, welcome them aboard Noah's ark. Hand out name tags and comment on their animal costumes. Show them into the kitchen, or another room, where you will have laid out a long piece of butcher paper or a poster board with a big rainbow on it. Encourage all of the children to color the rainbow with crayons or markers. Provide some animal pictures and coloring books to color as well.

Little ones may quickly lose interest in coloring, so let them play with the stuffed animals and other toys that you have made available. Some children may want to come back to the entrance to play in the ark again.

Let older children make thumb print animals. Provide construction paper and ink pads. Help the guests put their thumbprints on the paper and then use markers to add features to the animals.

2. Animal games

Gather the children into a circle and ask them to sit down. Say, "I see many special animals with us today. Isn't God great to make so many different kinds of wonderful animals? Let's see what animals we have here."

Ask each child what animal he is representing and ask him to make the animal's sound. Then, lead the children on an animal parade around the room. Play children's music while the children are marching.

Lead the children back to where they were sitting to play the animal guessing game. Tell the children that you are thinking of an animal that has big, tall ears and a fluffy tail. Ask if anyone can guess what it is. After they have guessed, tell them to get up and pretend they are rabbits. Continue this game using animals such as a lion, a chicken, a dog, an elephant, or a monkey. Ask some of the children to think of animals to add to the game.

You may want to play one or two of these games:

Ring the animals—Set several large stuffed animals about three feet away from where the children are standing. Mark a line that the children must stand behind. Give them a large ring or hoop to try to throw over the animals.

Animal cracker game—Fill a bowl with animal crackers and let each child pick one. Have the child stand up and act like the animal that he has chosen. When the group guesses the animal, the child is free to eat the cracker.

Animal hunt—Before the party, hide small plastic animals in a room other than the party room or in the backyard. You can purchase inexpensive plastic animals at toy stores and party stores. Give each child an empty favor bag with his name on it and let the children search for the animals as they would in an Easter egg hunt. Set a limit as to how many animals one child may collect. The number that each child can find depends on how many you want to buy. Be sure that the children are aware of the limit. Once a child has found his limit, ask her to come over and sit down in a circle to play with her animals.

After all the children have collected their animals and have sat down, tell them to put their animals back into their sacks and to put their sacks behind them. Let another adult collect the bags and put them on a shelf until playing time.

While you are sitting in the circle, play a rain game. Lead the children in clapping lightly to make the sound of a light rain. Begin clapping louder and louder. You can also pat on the floor in front of you with your hands. Lead the children to make the rain soft, then heavy, then back to soft again. You can also make some loud claps of thunder by smacking your hands together abruptly. After a little rainmaking, sing the song "Rain, Rain Go Away."

3. Story time

Tell the story of Noah. Emphasize that Noah trusted God and that we should too. Lead the children in hand motions as you go. For instance, when you are talking about Noah building the ark, let the children pretend they are hammering and sawing. As you tell about Noah gathering the animals into the ark, you can "walk" fingers on your right hand up your left arm, just as the animals walked into the ark. When it rains in the story, make your fingers wiggle as you move your hands in a downward motion to look like rain. As you tell about the dove that Noah sent out to find land, connect your hands by the thumbs and flap your fingers. To represent the rainbow, let everyone put their hands together over their heads with their arms arched in the shape of a rainbow. If you do not feel comfortable telling the story, ask a friend or a children's Sunday school teacher to tell the story.

Here is an example of how you may want to tell the story:

The Bible tells us about a man named Noah. He was a man who loved and trusted God. He lived in a time when people were very, very bad. Most people didn't love or care about the God who had made them. The people became so bad and wicked that God was sorry He had made them and He knew He must clean up the world from their bad ways.

The people had 120 years to decide to turn to God. You see, God came to Noah and said that He was going to send a flood. He told Noah to build a large boat, called an ark, to provide protection for the animals and Noah's family. Noah trusted and obeyed God. He tried to warn the bad people, but they didn't listen; they just laughed. They did not trust God.

It took Noah 120 years to build the ark. When it was finished, God brought two of every kind of animal aboard the ark and closed the door. The only people in the ark were Noah, his wife, his three sons, and their wives.

Then it started to rain. The rain lasted for a long time and water covered the entire earth. When the rain stopped, Noah had to wait for the water to go down before he could leave the ark. He sent out a dove to see if there was any dry land. One time the dove came back with a branch of a tree, so Noah knew that the water must be going down. The second time that Noah sent the dove out, he did not return, and Noah knew it was time to leave the ark.

When Noah's family came out of the ark, they thanked God. God promised never to cover the earth with a flood again, and He sealed His promise by putting a rainbow in the sky. When we see the rainbow, it reminds us that God keeps His promises. Noah trusted God and we can too.

Now lead the children in acting out the story. Pretend to be Noah and let the children be the animals. Let the parents who are present at the party participate if they would like.

4. Lunch or snacks and cake

Unless you have enough small tables and chairs for the children, consider letting the children eat on a tablecloth spread on the floor or let them eat outside on the porch.

5. Rainbow craft

You will need to prepare a few things ahead of time for the rainbow craft. Use a compass to draw circles with an 8-inch radius. Cut out the circles and cut each circle in half. You will need a semicircle for each guest. Use the compass again, and cut out circles of felt in three different colors. Use an 8-inch radius for one color, a 6-inch radius for the second color, and a 4-inch radius for the third color. Cut out the circles and cut them in half as you did the white circles.

Give each child a white poster board semicircle and one semicircle of each color of felt. Help the children glue the felt to the poster board, starting with the largest piece and ending with the smallest. The result will be a tricolor rainbow. Tape the rainbow to a coat hanger, lining up the flat side of the rainbow with the bottom of the hanger.

Next, give the children two cardboard clouds and let them glue cotton balls on the clouds. Attach the clouds to the ends of the rainbow with tape, glue, or staples. Show the children how the mobiles can hang on a door knob or from the ceiling. Let them get up and put their mobiles in their bags and then ask them to come back and be seated.

6. Open presents

Use masking tape to make a rainbow semicircle on the floor or carpet. Tell the children to sit on the tape to make a "people rainbow." Tell them that everyone must stay seated to be able to watch the birthday boy open his presents. Call out a type of animal and let the children who are dressed as that animal come forward and give their gifts to the birthday child. Once they have presented their gifts, they should return to the rainbow and be seated.

If this is not a birthday party, skip this activity and begin with play time.

7. Free play time

Tell the children that they may play in the ark or with the stuffed animals and any other toys you have made available. Put away any of the birthday presents that you do not want the children to play with. Let your child choose at least one new gift that he will allow his guests to play with and enjoy. This encourages your child to develop a sense of sharing on a day that could easily build selfishness.

If you have mostly older children (ages four and five), you may want to provide a more organized activity. Consider giving them clay or play dough to make animal figures. Let them use animal-shaped cookie cutters. Make your own dough and let the children take their creations home. Here is a simple recipe:

No-Cook Play Dough

1 cup white flour
$\frac{1}{2}$ cup salt
2 tablespoons vegetable oil
1 teaspoon alum (You can find alum in drugstores.)
food coloring
$\frac{1}{2}$ cup water

Mix the first four ingredients together. Add several drops of food coloring to the water. Gradually add small amounts of water to the mixture until it has the consistency of bread dough. You may not use all of the water. Store in an airtight container or plastic bag.

FOOD:

Decide whether you want to provide lunch or simply cake and ice cream. Choose food from this list to fit your decision:

Animal sandwiches—Use cookie cutters to cut the kids' favorite sandwiches into animal shapes.
Banana or apple slices
Pretzels or chips
Blue drink mix or punch
Rainbow cake and cupcakes—Use an 8- or 9-inch round cake. (You

only need one layer, so use the rest of the batter for cupcakes.) Cut the cake down the middle. Ice the top of one half using white creamy icing. Put the other layer on top of the iced layer. Place the cake, cut side down, on a serving platter. Frost all exposed sides of the cake.

You will need about two cups of icing. Place colored candies in rows to form the different colors of the rainbow. Jelly beans, gumdrops, or sprinkles will work well. Keep in mind the age group you will be serving; do not serve jelly beans to young children who could easily choke on them. This cake makes about eight servings. You can make two cakes or decorate cupcakes for the children and save the cake for the adults. You could make a fun project for older children by letting them decorate their cupcakes with the colored candies.

Ice cream—Serve rainbow sherbert.

FAVORS: Pick and choose from this list

1. Favor bags—Buy colored gift bags at a card shop or a craft store. Give each child a different color bag. Write the guests' names on white paper clouds and attach them to the bags.
2. Plastic animals found in the animal hunt game
3. Rainbow mobile
4. Rainbow or animal stickers
5. Small plastic boats
6. Rainbow pencils
7. Animal crackers
8. Small paperback book telling the story of Noah's Ark. You may be able to find these books at a Christian bookstore.
9. Sunglasses
10. Animal noses—Some party stores carry animal noses as packaged party favors for the children to wear.

* 2 *

Dalmation Sensation

Hot diggity dog! It's a dalmatian party full of canine fun! As children arrive, they will make their own dog tags and receive dog ears. A spot game and doggy songs make this party a howling success. The children will have dog food made of trail mix and bone-shaped sandwiches for snacks. Danny the Dalmatian will teach the children about how God has made each of us with unique and special qualities.

➡ **Suggested Size:** 5 to 12 children
Suggested Time of Day: morning or afternoon
Type: boys, girls, or both

YOU WILL NEED:

- Poster boards
- Small white sacks
- Construction paper
- Tape
- Sock puppet
- White and black felt
- Towels
- Foil and name tags
- Favors
- Balloons and crepe paper streamers
- Large box

INVITATIONS:

The invitations will look like dalmatian puppets. Use white lunch sacks or small white gift bags to make the dog. When the sack is folded, there is a flap that forms the bottom of the sack when it's in use. This flap will be the puppet's face. Cut a small black circle from construction paper to be the dog's nose and glue it on the face of the puppet. Make a red tongue and place it so that it is slightly hanging out of the dog's mouth. Use black construction paper for the ears and eyes. Draw black spots at random on the front and back of the dog. Put the invitation information on an index card inside the sack. You will need to use large envelopes for mailing the invitation or hand deliver them. Be sure to draw dots on the envelope too.

You can make a simple alternative invitation from plain white note card stationery, drawing a dalmatian face on the card. On the back of the card put the party information. Put it in an envelope that you have decorated with black spots and mail it.

Write the party information as follows:

It's a Dalmation Celebration!

For: _____

Dog Date: _____

Dog Time: _____

Dog House: _____

RSVP to the master: _____

WE'RE GONNA HAVE A HOWLING GOOD TIME!

DECORATIONS:

The colors for the dalmatian party are white, black, and red. You may be able to find white plates and balloons that have black spots on them. If not, you can make your own spotted decorations, using a black magic marker on white paper goods. Use red disposable plastic bowls for the trail mix "dog food." As one of the favors, you could give each child an inexpensive plastic cereal bowl with his name painted on the side to look like a dog food bowl.

Cut large black spots out of poster boards or construction paper and tape them on the walls of the party room. Make them all different sizes and shapes. (A dalmatian's spots are rarely perfect circles.) Using a red marker, write *Welcome* on one white poster board and copy Psalm 139:14 on another. Decorate the posters with black spots. Hang alternating black and white streamers from the tops of doorways.

Make a doghouse for the entrance. Use a large appliance box from a washer or dryer or TV. Cut a door, rounded at the top, in the front and in the back of the box for the kids to walk or crawl through. Use red poster boards to make the roof of the doghouse.

SCHEDULE: 1½ hours

15 minutes—Arrive, make dog collars, put on costumes
20 minutes—Dog songs and dog games
20 minutes—Snack time
15 minutes—Danny the Dalmatian
10 minutes—Open presents
10 minutes—Play time

ACTIVITIES:

1. Arrive, make dog collars, put on costumes

Greet your guests at the door with a howling "Hello" and give them their dog ears. You can make these ears using black felt and a white cap, headband or visor. Purchase black felt from a fabric store and cut it into oval dog ear shapes. Attach the ears to the sides of either the cap, headband, or visor using a hot glue gun or craft glue.

After guests have put on their ears, show them to the room where the collars are being made. Children will make the collars from strips of construction paper about two inches wide. Provide washable markers, stickers, glue and sequins for the children to use to decorate their collars.

For the dog tags, take 3-inch circles cut from poster board and let the children cover them with foil. Cut name tags out of plain white stickers and attach them to the circles. Punch a hole at the top of each dog tag and let the child put a short string through the hole. Tie the ends of the string in a knot and put the collar through the loop of string. Put the collar around the child's neck and tape it so that it is loose. You don't want the collar to fall off; on the other hand, you do want the collar to pull apart if someone yanks on it. Remind the children that they should not pull on another person's collar.

Once they have finished making their collars, let them try on their white dog costumes. For the dog costume, purchase white felt at a fabric store. You will need about ⅓ of a yard per child. Cut a hole in the center of each rectangle of white felt. The children will wear the felt like a tunic. You can attach ribbon or elastic to the sides to hold them together, but it is not necessary. The children may ask you, "Where are the dog's spots?" Tell them to wait and see.

2. Dog games and songs

Gather the children together in a circle and tell them that they make super dogs but that they need some spots if they are going to be dalmatians. Before the party, cut out 3-inch black felt spots (about 12 spots per guest). Stick or glue a small tab of velcro on the back of the spots to help them stick to the felt. Use only the rough half of the velcro.

Explain to the children that when you say to begin, they will start putting spots on the other dogs. Each child must put a spot on all the other children at the party. Tell them to make sure that they do not miss anyone. The spots should stay on the costumes if the velcro side is pressed onto the white felt. You may need to help make sure that each child receives a good amount of spots.

Now the children can play one or more of the following games:

Pretend Doggies—Let the children pretend that they are doggies. Give each child a small towel and tell them that these are their doggy beds. Let them curl up on their beds and ask the children if they can think of some other things that dogs do. They may say things such as barking, walking, running, begging, jumping, eating, howling, rolling over, and playing dead. Let the children act out each action that they name. They will have a great time barking and running, so allow them to get a little loud and silly.

When you want them to calm down, tell them that it is time for the doggies to go back to sleep. Have them return to their towels and curl up or sit. Give each child a pat on the head and tell them, "Good Doggy."

The Dog Bone game—The children will remain seated except for the one selected to be the Dog. Have the Dog sit with his eyes closed, facing away from the group. Put a bone behind the Dog's back, in full view of the others. The bone can be any object close to the size of a bone or you can use a dog biscuit. Choose one child to sneak up and take the bone. Then he returns to his seat and hides the bone behind him. The whole group then chants, "Doggie, Doggie where's your bone?" The Dog turns around, and he has three chances to guess who has the bone. If the Dog guesses incorrectly, the group says no. If the Dog guesses where the bone is, they applaud. Either way, the child who stole the bone becomes the dog next. This game works best with four and five year old children.

Dog tag—Play tag, but have the children crawl instead of run. The safe zone can be the dog house you made for the entrance, but only two people can be there at a time. When a child arrives at the safe zone, then the child who has been there the longest must leave.

Newspaper relay—Since dogs sometimes bring in the paper, have a newspaper relay. Give each child two pieces of white typing paper rolled up to look like a newspaper. Separate into two teams. The object of the game is for each "dog" to carry the newspaper in his mouth while crawling on the floor to a designated spot, around it, and back to tag the next teammate. The first team to have every player finish his route wins.

After playing games, lead the children in some doggy songs. Start off by singing "Oh Where, Oh Where, Has My Little Dog Gone." "Bingo" is another popular favorite with the children. Next, lead the children in barking some old familiar tunes. Use songs like "Row, Row, Row Your Boat," "Yankee Doodle," and "Happy Birthday," barking instead of singing the words.

Have the children stand up for the next song. This song is sung to the tune of "Father Abraham Had Many Sons." If you do not know this tune, your children's minister or youth minister at church may be able to help.

Dalmation Doggies

Dalmatian doggies have many spots,
Many spots have dalmatian doggies.
I have some of them and so do you,
So let's just go like this:

With the right . . .
(Hold right arm up and move it back and forth)

(Repeat first stanza)

With the right . . .
With the left . . .
(Hold both arms up and move them back and forth)

(Repeat first stanza)

With the right . . .
With the left . . .
And the right . . .
(While continuing to move both arms, lift one leg up and down, bending at the knee)

(Repeat first stanza)

With the right . . .
With the left . . .

And the right . . .
And the left . . .
(Arms still moving, march in place)

(Repeat first stanza)

With the right . . .
With the left . . .
And the right . . .
And the left . . .
And the tail . . . .
(As they continue the other motions, have them try to wiggle their tails)

3. Snack time

Tell the children that it is feeding time and that since they are dogs, you are going to give them some dog food to eat. You may hear some giggles, but other children may look worried. Just smile and lead them into the kitchen.

Tell the children to find a place on the floor and then put a paper place mat in front of them. Give each child an empty bowl with his name on it. As I mentioned earlier, you may want to purchase some inexpensive plastic cereal bowls and paint the names on the sides so they can take them home as favors. Now bring out a big grocery sack or a box labeled *Dog Food* full of trail mix. Tell the children that this is their dog food and pour it into their bowls.

Provide dog bone sandwiches (see the food section) and apple juice. Serve a dalmatian cake and chocolate chip ice cream for dessert. For fun, call the ice cream "Dalmatian Delight."

4. Danny the Dalmation

After the children finish, tell them to gather in the other room to meet Danny the Dalmatian, a sock puppet. Make Danny before the party using an athletic sock and some black felt. Sew or glue a black pom pom to the toe of the sock for Danny's nose. Attach felt ears to the sides and use buttons for the eyes. Use some red material on the underside for the tongue. Color spots on the sock with a black marker. Your thumb will move back and forth in the heel of the sock to make Danny's mouth open and close.

If you have a stuffed dalmatian, you may want to use it instead of the sock puppet. You could also use a sack puppet like the ones described in the invitation section.

Make a dramatic entrance by hiding Danny behind your back and telling the children to say "Hello Danny" in order for him to come out. When Danny comes out, have him give a big, howling "Hel-looooooo!"

Here's what Danny should say:

Welcome to the party, boys and girls. I'm so glad you came to help wish _____ a happy birthday. Birthdays are special. Did you know that dalmatian doggies are special too? We all have spots, but not one of us is like the other. You see, God gave us each a unique set of spots. Some of us have many spots, some of us have very few. Our spots are all placed in different patterns and places. We are each a special masterpiece.

Did you know that you are a masterpiece too? You each have unique talents and abilities and interests that are special to you. Some of you are great singers, some are great painters, some can read really well, others may have a special way of showing kindness to friends. God can use you each in a special way.

I'm thankful for my special spots. I hope that you will thank God for the special way He made you.

5. Open presents

Tell the children to sit on their towels again. Ask the birthday child to come sit in a chair and open the presents. After he opens each present, let him bark a "thank you" to the giver.

6. Play time

Let the children play with some toys that you have made available. Bring out a couple of balls and sticks and play fetch. Use a hoop to let the children jump through and do tricks. Play some more dog tag. You will find that the children love to pretend and will have a grand time pretending to be dogs.

FOOD:

Dog food—Make trail mix consisting of pretzels, raisins, cereal, and M&M's or use your own combination.

Dog bones—Make your child's favorite sandwiches and cut them in the shape of a dog bone. Don't be too concerned about making the shapes perfect; remember, these are to be eaten, not admired.

Apple juice

Dog cake and cupcakes—Bake one layer of a round cake using your favorite recipe or mix. Use the rest of the mix for cupcakes. Put one cupcake on the center of the cake to form the dog's snout. Ice the cake with white icing. Use oval chocolate cookies for the eyes, a black gumdrop for the nose, Ding Dongs for the ears, and red licorice or candy for the tongue. Randomly place chocolate kisses or chocolate candies for the dog's spots.

The cupcakes will be miniature versions of the dog cake. Use broken chocolate cookies instead of Ding Dongs for the ears. Decorate the rest of the cupcake with the same ingredients you used on the large cake.

Chocolate chip ice cream

FAVORS: Pick and choose from the following:

1. Favor bags—Make them from white lunch sacks or gift bags. Use a black marker to spot them.
2. Dog food bowls with the guests' names painted on them. You can buy inexpensive plastic bowls at the grocery store or a discount store, or you can save a few whipped topping tubs. Start saving now.
3. Dalmation costumes
4. Dog ears on a headband, cap, or visor
5. Balloons
6. Small packages of chocolate sandwich cookies or chocolate chip cookies
7. White plastic cups or any white item such as mirrors, combs, hair bows, or sunglasses, on which you can paint black spots
8. Small book about dogs
9. Plastic dog toys—These pet toys make fun trinkets for children too.
10. Dog collars

* 3 *

Farmer Party

It's a Hoe Down on the old farm! The kids will have a grand time as they play country games such as sack races, wheelbarrow races, and three-legged races. They will also learn about farm life by gathering apples, milking a cow, and going on a hayride. Farm snacks and a pig cake will make snack time a lot of fun. The theme is found in Genesis 8:22: God promises that there will always be a seedtime and harvest.

➡ **Suggested Size:**   5 to 12 kids
   Suggested Time of Day: morning or afternoon
   Type: boys, girls, or both

This party is best held outdoors. Your backyard could be perfect, or you can check your area to see if there are any local farms that host parties. A local park would be another super location. If it rains, never fear—this party will work just as well indoors.

YOU WILL NEED:

- Hay
- Poster board
- Latex or rubber gloves
- Old clothes and boots
- Bandannas
- Burlap fabric
- Balloons

- Favors
- Food
- Newspaper
- Brown paper bags
- Yardsticks and yarn
- Plastic farm animals

INVITATIONS:

The invitations will look like the face of a farmer. Cut a white 3-inch circle for the head and cut out a burlap hat and glue it at the top. Use markers to draw facial features. Glue yarn under the hat for hair and tie a small strip of bandanna around the neck. Write the party information on the back. Send the invitation in a business size envelope. Here is how the information should read:

```
Farmer _____ (child's name) _____ invites you to . . .
A birthday hoe down!
Time: _____
Farm location: _____
Hoe down date: _____
RSVP: _____
       HOPE YOU CAN COME FOR SOME COTTON PICKIN' FUN.
```

DECORATIONS:

There is a bushel full of ideas for decorating for this party. Start off by transforming your door into a barn door. Don't worry, you will not have to take the door off its hinges. Use plain red wrapping paper to wrap your front door. Cut out white poster board slats to cross in the front. Place some bales of hay by the front door. Contact a feed store to buy the hay.

Your theme colors will be red and blue. Use these colors for balloons, streamers, and paper goods. Set apples all around the party room or outdoors where the party will be located. Make sure they are washed and be sure to set trash cans around for disposal of apple cores. Bandannas make another colorful decoration. Buy them by the bundle or buy bandanna fabric and cut your own. Tie the bandannas everywhere. You can also give these as favors to the children as they arrive.

Farm animals make another great decoration. Use farm animal pictures, books with animal pictures, and any stuffed farm animals you have to set around the party rooms. Put bandannas around the necks of the stuffed animals.

Do you have any overalls? Wear them or hang them on the wall. Or put a stuffed bear in them and set him on top of the bail of hay. If you don't own any, you may be able to find an inexpensive pair at a thrift store. Checked shirts and western shirts also add to the farm look.

On your food table, use red checked tablecloths. You can find inexpensive plastic ones at party stores or grocery stores. Cut name tags in the shape of an apple from red construction paper.

SCHEDULE: 1½ hours

15 minutes—Arrive, horseshoes, stuff the scarecrow
20 minutes—Farm games
20 minutes—Chow down
20 minutes—Gathering the harvest
10 minutes—Open presents
5 minutes—Free play

ACTIVITIES:

1. Arrive, horseshoes, stuff the scarecrow

As children arrive, give them a bandanna, pin on their name tags, and let them join the others for a game of horseshoes. You will need to have another adult helping with the horseshoe game while you greet guests. Make horseshoes out of colored poster boards, taping pennies or washers to the two ends and middle of each horseshoe to give it some weight. You can use a small pole or let the kids try to throw the horseshoes into a basket.

Another activity the kids can enjoy as they arrive is stuffing the scarecrow. Draw a face on a brown paper grocery sack and use it for the scarecrow's head. Use an old pair of men's pants for legs, a shirt for the body, gloves for hands, and boots for feet. Let the kids help stuff the scarecrow with crumpled up paper. As a group, put the complete scarecrow together and then seat him against a wall for decoration.

Yardstick horses can also be fun for the kids during arrival time. Make the horses using poster board and yarn for the head and mane. Let the kids play on these until you are ready for some organized games. It may be hard to get the kids off the horses because they are such fun. Tell them that the horses must go back in the barn for a while, and put the horses out of sight until you are ready to use them again.

2. Farm games

These races and games are some old favorites that the kids will love. Although it would be best to have the party outside, these games can be played inside just as easily. Just move your furniture to the sides of the room to provide some wide open space. Encourage all of the kids to race at the same time instead of running a relay. Cheer them on and applaud all who finish. No prizes are necessary, but if you want to give them, give a prize to everyone who finishes.

Many games and activities are presented here, so pick and choose the ones that best suit your group and schedule.

Sack races—Down on the farm they would use feed sacks or potato sacks for this race, but in the city we use pillow cases. Let each child have his own sack. Everyone steps into his sack and waits behind the starting line. When an adult shouts "go!" the kids race by hopping in their sacks until they cross the finish line. If you have more than ten guests or varied age groups, then you may want to have a couple of separate races.

Three-legged race—Pair each child with a partner who is about the same size. Loosely tie one child's leg to her partner's leg with a bandanna. Each pair starts at the starting line together and runs to the finish line. If they fall down, they just get up and keep going. Let the kids practice walking around with their partners before the race begins.

Wheelbarrow race—This race should be shorter. Pair the children so that a strong one partners with a small one. The small one can act as the wheelbarrow; he walks on his hands while his partner holds his feet. Let the kids have fun trying this race even if they cannot make it across the finish line.

Play and sing—"The Farmer in the Dell" is a kid's favorite. Have the children stand in a circle and hold hands. Remember the words:

> The farmer in the dell,
> The farmer in the dell,
> Hi ho, the dairy-o,
> The farmer in the dell.
>
> verse 2: The farmer takes a wife.
> verse 3: The wife takes a child.
> verse 4: The child takes a nurse.
> verse 5: The nurse takes a dog.
> verse 6: The dog takes a cat.
> verse 7: The cat takes a rat.

verse 8: The rat takes the cheese.
verse 9: The cheese stands alone.

The children standing in the circle hold hands and walk to the left. One child stands in the middle of the circle as the farmer. He chooses someone from the circle as his wife during the second verse. On the third verse, the wife chooses another child to join them in the center as the child. The game continues on until the cheese is chosen. On the last verse the children stop marching and clap as those in the middle go back to the circle. The cheese stays in the middle as the new farmer.

Don't forget the old favorite "Old McDonald Had a Farm." You can change the name Old McDonald to your child's name, singing, "Farmer _____."

Hayrides—Put some hay in a small red wagon or wheelbarrow and let some of the other adults give the children hayrides around the yard.

Tug of war—Get a large twine rope and divide the kids into two groups. Stand in the middle and tell the kids that the team that pulls the other team past you is the winning team.

Dress-up relay—Provide two sets of clothes including: pants, shirts, boots and hats. The clothes should be larger than the children's size since they will be putting them on over their clothes. Have the children stand in two lines. The first child on each team will run to the pile of clothes for her team and put them on over her clothes. She does not need to fasten the buttons or zippers. Once she gets all four items on, she should take them off and put them back in a pile and run back to the line so the next person can go. You will need one adult to help with the clothes and another to tend the relay line.

Petting zoo—Check the yellow pages to see if there are any petting zoos in the area that will bring animals to your home. Expense will be a big factor, but if you can work out a reasonable price, the kids would love it!

3. Chow down

You will be serving farm snacks and a pig cake (described in the food section). I suggest laying some quilts or red checked tablecloths on the ground to have a picnic. If the weather is bad, move the kitchen table to the side of the room and have a picnic on the kitchen floor.

4. Gathering the harvest

After everyone is finished eating, gather everyone together and ask them to sit down on a quilt or blanket. Ask the kids if they know some of the jobs that farmers have. They may mention milking cows, planting seeds, picking apples and corn, or baling hay. Ask them if they know who really makes all the wonderful crops to grow. Make a poster with pictures cut from magazines of different fruits and vegetables. Print the words from Genesis 8:22 on the poster.

Tell the kids:

The Bible says that the seed and the harvest would never stop. God has made a wonderful cycle. The farmer plants the seeds in spring, and by fall, the crops have grown. We call the crops that grow the *harvest*. God is the one we depend on for the crops to grow. Do you suppose the farmers thank God when they have a good harvest? Shouldn't we thank Him too?

Pray with the children or allow one or two of them to thank God for the harvest and the crops.

Next, teach the kids about farm life through games and activities. While you are talking to the kids, ask some of the parents to distribute apples made of construction paper all around the yard. Make enough so that each child can gather five. Attach a small candy to each apple to make the game more exciting. When you give the signal, the kids will hunt for apples in the yard. Their limit is five. Tell them that after they have found five, they are to come and sit down. Let them eat at least one of their candies. Younger ones may need some help finding their five apples.

Next, try milking cows. Hold on. Don't worry, you don't need a cow in your backyard for this activity. You may want to play this game outside or over the kitchen sink. Use a latex or rubber glove and make a pin prick in each finger tip. Pour a small amount of milk into the gloves. Twist the top of the glove and hold it tight while you let the children take turns squirting the milk out of the fingers of the glove into a pail. With older kids (four and five years old) you could make this a relay game to see which team could fill their bucket to a certain level first. Put a white poster board with black spots above the area where the glove will be. Attach a tail to one side of the poster.

While some of the kids are busy milking cows, you can let others try their hand at fishing. Make fishing poles with sticks and attach string to one end. Put a magnet at the other end of the string. Cut out cardboard fish and put a paper clip on each fish. Put the fish in an empty inflatable pool. You can give prizes for the fish they catch.

Churning butter is another fun farm activity. Put about a pint of cream into a jar with a screw-on lid. It is best to use cream that is several days old. Shake the cream gently until small lumps of butter form. Let the children take turns at the churn. Tell the kids how butter is churned on the farm. If you have a picture of an old churn, show it to them. Put the butter into a bowl and work it into a lump with a spatula or wooden spoon, squeezing out the remaining buttermilk. Add a pinch of salt. Continue kneading the butter with the spoon until it forms a smooth lump. Serve the butter on crackers as a special treat.

5. Open presents

Again ask the kids to return to the quilt to watch the birthday child open presents. If you are outside, let the birthday child sit in the hayride wagon or a special chair so everyone can see. Call out each child's name to give their gift by saying, "Farmer _____."

6. Free play

The last few minutes of the party should be left to free play. Allow the children to play with the toys that you have made available as well as one or two of the presents. Bring out the yardstick horses and give the children their favors at this time.

FOOD:

Serve farm fresh food in small wooden produce baskets lined with a bandanna. Here are some suggested refreshments.

Apples, peaches, or berries
Carrot slices
Hard-boiled eggs
Homemade bread or biscuits
Cheese and ham slices
Pig Cake—Bake your favorite round cake and use the rest of the mix for cupcakes. Put one overturned cupcake on top of the round cake for the snout. Use pink icing to cover the cake. Decorate with chocolate cookies for the eyes and raisins for the snout. Cut another cupcake down the middle and use each half, with the cut side down, for the ears.

FAVORS:

1. Favor sacks—Use brown paper lunch sacks gathered at the top and tied with strips of bandanna or red ribbon.

2. Straw farmer hats and bandannas
3. Prizes from the fish pond
4. Plastic farm animals
5. Vegetable seeds and a planting tool
6. White plastic cup with cow spots painted on it, labeled *Milk Cup*
7. Shiny red apple
8. Balloons
9. Yardstick ponies

* 4 *

Dandy Dolly Party

Invite the girls to bring their favorite doll to this frilly party! The girls will dress up their dolls and give them a fancy dolly tea party. Paper doll sewing cards will make a special craft for the young ladies. When the dolls are finished, the girls can enjoy some delightful dolly games. The theme will come from Mark 10:14–16: Jesus loves the little children.

➡ **Suggested Size:** 3 to 10 kids
Suggested Time of Day: morning or afternoon
Type: girls

YOU WILL NEED:

- Poster board
- Plastic tea set
- Yarn
- Fabric scraps

- Balloons and crepe paper streamers
- Favors
- Food

INVITATIONS:

The invitations will be 7-inch cardboard paper dolls with the party information written on the back. Use poster board to cut out a paper doll. Attach yellow or brown yarn for hair and cut fabric scraps to make the clothes. On the back write this information:

IT'S A DANDY DOLLY TEA PARTY!

Join _____ as she celebrates her
                    (child's name)

[2nd, 3rd, etc.]   birthday.

Time: _____

Date: _____

Place: _____

RSVP: _____

Please bring along your favorite baby doll for tea.

Make sure the paper doll is no more than four inches wide so it can fit into a business size envelope. Instead of fabric for the paper doll clothes, you may choose to make paper outfits out of construction paper. Put tabs on the edges just like real paper dolls.

DECORATIONS:

Think pink! Your theme colors will be light pink and dark pink. Purchase paper goods, balloons, and streamers in these colors. For more decorations, set out every doll that you have in the house. Borrow friends' dolls as well. Put the dolls on coffee tables, end tables, couches, TVs, and chairs.

For the front door, make a collage of doll pictures cut from magazines. Leave a space in the center to write the word *Welcome*.

On the walls, tape paper dolls and their clothes. Set up doll-sized tables for tea. You can use children's tables or coffee tables and shoe boxes for chairs. Use lace or pink plastic tablecloths cut down to size. Put a small plastic flower arrangement in the center of each table. Seat about four guest's dolls per table. Purchase an inexpensive plastic tea set to be used for the party. Do not set the table until it is time for tea.

SCHEDULE: 1½ hours

20 minutes—Dress up dolls
20 minutes—Tea party
20 minutes—Kid snacks
10 minutes—Doll sewing cards
10 minutes—Open presents
10 minutes—Free play or sewing cards

ACTIVITIES:

1. Dress up dolls

As the young ladies arrive, help them with name tags for both the girls and their dolls. Ask each girl to tell you her dolly's name and how she got that name. Lead the children into the beauty shop so that they can get their dollies ready for tea. They will actually be playing dress up with their dollies.

From the remnant section at a fabric store, purchase all sorts of fancy material. Look for netting, chiffons, laces, metallics, and other special fabrics. Cut them into strips so that the girls can use them for bows or belts or scarves for their dolls. Provide beads and string for the girls to make jewelry. Jewelry making is best for 3-5 year olds.

You will want to have plenty of doll-sized hairbrushes to style the doll's hair. These can be purchased at a toy store and used for favors at the end of the party. Look for doll-sized straw hats and let the girls decorate them. You may find these hats at craft stores. Consider having some girl's dress-up clothes so that the girls can play dress up too. You can purchase dress up clothes at thrift stores or make your own using remnant fabric.

2. Tea Party

Introduce the dolls to each other by name. Let the girls seat their dolls and serve them tea. Use water in the teapot instead of tea and shortbread cookies for tea cookies. This is an unstructured time; just sit back and let the girls play. Let their imaginations work.

If you feel the need for some structure, sing circle songs with the girls and dolls. Songs such as "Ring Around the Rosie" and "London Bridge" can be lots of fun when dolls play too.

3. Kid snacks

After about twenty minutes of pretend, tell the girls to join you in the kitchen for a snack for themselves. Serve finger sandwiches or doll-shaped sandwiches and enjoy a beautiful doll cake for dessert (see food section).

4. Sewing cards

Make poster board dolls that are about eight inches tall and punch holes around the edges before the party. Let the girls color the dolls, then give them yarn to string through the holes in the dolls. Be sure to make a knot on one end of the yarn and put tape on the other end so it will go through the holes with ease. You could also use inexpensive colored shoelaces. Demonstrate to the girls how to do the sewing and do not expect perfection, especially if they are younger girls.

After the girls are finished sewing, put their sewing cards by their favor bags. Play some of these games if you have extra time:

Simon Says—Let the dolls do the actions that Simon says.

Pin the Doll Clothes on the Dolly—This game works on the same concept as "Pin the Tail on the Donkey," using a cut-out doll and paper clothing instead of a donkey and a tail.

Hide and Seek—Have each girl hide her doll and return to the center of the room. After all of the dolls are hidden, each girl should try and find a doll other than her own. Once all of the dolls have been found, return the dolls to their owners and play again.

Sing—Sing "I'm A Little Teapot," making the dollies do the motions.

After playing a few games, ask the girls to join you in a circle on the floor. Let them hold their dolls while you talk to them.

Say something like this:

Dolls are sure fun, aren't they? I know when I used to play with dolls, I would pretend that I was the mommy and my doll was my child. Do you play that way too?

Did you know that there is a story in the Bible about Jesus and mommies and their children?

One day, several mommies wanted to take their children to see Jesus. As they came nearer and nearer, the disciples (Jesus' friends) saw them coming. They knew that Jesus was very tired, so they thought they would help Him out by telling the mommies to go home. When Jesus saw the mommies and the children, He had a different idea. He said, Let the little children come to Me, and do not forbid them; for of such is the kingdom of God. How special those children must have felt! Just think, God's Son wanted to see them and bless them and hold them! He knew that their simple faith was special.

5. Open presents

Set the dolls in a circle and give each doll a present to hold. The guests will sit behind their dolls. Call out a doll's name. When a name is called, the girl with that doll will hand her gift to the birthday girl.

If this is not a birthday party, play "I Spy" by setting the dolls in a circle and having a child say, "I spy a doll that has a white button." The kids can ask yes or no questions to try to determine which doll is being described.

6. Free play

Let the girls play with the dolls or whatever toys you have set out for play. Give the girls some items to encourage their imaginations, such as toy doctor's kits or doll furniture and accessories to play house. As favors you may want to give each of the guests a miniature doctor's kit. See the favors section for details.

FOOD:

Finger sandwiches

Fruit slices

Cheese slices—If you have a gingerbread boy cookie cutter, use it for cutting the cheese slices.

Pink lemonade

Doll cake—Using a greased metal mixing bowl or a mold from a cooking or craft store, bake your favorite cake recipe. You could even use a bundt pan. Let the cake cool for ten minutes, then invert the bowl and release the cake. The cake will be the skirt for your doll cake. Wash a fashion doll and put it in the center of the cake. It would be best if you can separate the doll at the waist. Some craft stores have half dolls for cakes like this. Ice the cake using pink icing. Cover the bodice of the doll as well. Use decorative icing at the bottom as trim.

FAVORS: Pick and choose

1. Favor sacks—Use pink or white gift sacks and draw a simple doll outline on the side. Punch two holes in the doll's hair and tie a ribbon through the holes to close the sack.
2. Doll tea cups—These are available at toy stores.
3. Doll brush and comb set
4. Hair bows—Make your own bows using pink ribbon and netting. Cut a square of netting, gather it in the middle, and tie a bow around it with ribbon. Use a hot glue gun to attach the bow to a barrette.
5. Doll doctor kit—You can make your own kits complete with Band-Aids, tongue depressors, stethoscopes, and blood pressure monitors. Put all of the items in a small gift bag or shoe box.

    To make stethoscopes, you will need pipe cleaners and an egg carton. Connect two pipe cleaners together to make the tubes going to the ears. Attach another pipe cleaner to the center. The other end of the third pipe cleaner should be connected to a cup from the egg carton to make the chest piece.

To make a blood pressure monitor, use a small strip of fabric for the arm band and sew or glue some velcro onto the ends. Use some thick string to run from the arm band to the pump. For the pump, use a balloon with flour or a small amount of air in it. You can make the monitor by cutting out a cardboard circle and attaching it to the fabric strip.

To make a syringe, use a straw and a pipe cleaner. Make a circle with the end of the pipe cleaner. Cut the straw in half and place the pipe cleaner through the straw. Cut off excess pipe cleaner.

Include real Band-Aids and tongue depressors.

6. Store-bought paper dolls
7. Sewing cards
8. Balloons
9. Tea cookies
10. Small play purses
11. Decorated plastic knickknack boxes

* 5 *

Angelic Hosts

This heavenly party will take the children to new heights. Cloud hopping and trumpet blowing are all part of the fun. Don't forget the angel food cake! This angelic happening is glorious for anytime of the year, but it would make a super party around Christmas or Easter. The theme will come from Psalm 91:11: "For He shall give His angels charge over you, to keep you in all your ways."

➡ **Suggested Size:** 5 to 12 kids
Suggested Time of Day: morning or afternoon
Type: boys, girls, or both

YOU WILL NEED:

- Poster board
- Cotton balls
- Gold jewels and sequins
- White fabric or T-shirts
- Gold pipe cleaners
- Gold spray paint
- Favors
- Balloons and crepe paper streamers

INVITATIONS:

Make invitations in the shape of a cloud. Cut 4-inch by 6-inch clouds out of white poster board. Outline the clouds with silver or gold glitter. Pull apart a few cotton balls and glue them in the center of the cloud. Write the party information on the back.

Join the heavenly host
For an angelic party
To celebrate _____ (child's name) _____ birthday!
Glory Date: _____
Celestial Time: _____
Pearly Gate Address: _____
RSVP: _____

DECORATIONS:

Use several white poster boards to make large clouds as you did for the invitations. Hang the clouds with string from the ceiling. On one cloud copy Psalm 91. Make another cloud to serve as the welcome sign on the front door. Lay white sheets on the floor near the front door so that when the children arrive they feel like they are in the clouds. Purchase many white balloons. If you expect small children (two years old and under), then use helium balloons so that they will be out of reach of the little ones. If you know you will be having only older kids, place balloons all over the house, on the floors and tables. Hang white streamers from the tops of the doorways. Display any angels that you can find among your Christmas decorations.

SCHEDULE: 1½ hours

15 minutes—Arrive, become an angel
25 minutes—Games and songs
20 minutes—Snacks
15 minutes—Angel talk and craft
10 minutes—Open presents
5 minutes—Free play

ACTIVITIES:

1. Arrive, become an angel

As your guests arrive, greet them at the door and tell them that they are going to dress as an angel for the party. Give them a white men's T-shirt or a white poncho made from plain white cotton fabric. Help them put their outfits on and tell them to join the others in the kitchen to decorate their wings. Each child will receive a poster board pair of wings. Before the party, cut the poster board in wing shapes. You should be able to get two sets of wings from each board. In your garage or basement, lay the wings out on the floor and lightly paint them with gold spray. Be sure to do this a couple of days before the party so that the wings will have time to dry.

Let the children decorate their wings by putting stickers and jewels and sequins on them. For the jewels and sequins, pour a small amount of glue in a paper plate and let the children apply the glue using cotton swabs. The wings will need to dry, so put everyone's name on their wings and leave them in the kitchen during the party. You can pin the wings on the children at the end of the party for pictures.

Give them a halo to wear. Make the halo using gold pipe cleaners for the halo and the stem. Use a head band or poster board ring to hold the halo on their heads.

Once the children have received their halos, play star hopscotch. Use construction paper or poster boards to cut out 5-inch stars. You will need at least ten. Tape them to the floor in the shape of a hopscotch game. Let the kids play hopscotch on the stars. You may want to make more than one game so that more children can play at one time.

2. Games and songs

Gather the kids together for celestial games. I have listed many games here for you. Play as many as time permits.

Pillow cloud toss—Bring out about four small throw pillows for the cloud games. Tell the kids that the pillows are really clouds and let them try to throw the pillows into a laundry basket that is placed about two feet away. You can have several children throwing pillows at the same time. Remember that pillows are much heavier to the little ones than they are to us. Let them also try to toss the pillow through a ring or hoop.

You can also play a hot potato game passing the pillow around the circle. When you shout "storm cloud!" they must speed up the pace as they pass the cloud. Do not eliminate the children who drop the cloud. Just have them pick it up and continue. Slow the pace by saying "calm cloud."

Cotton ball races—Give everyone a plastic spoon and a cotton ball. This is not a relay. Line everyone up side by side, facing the finish line, and let them all go at the same time. Tell the children that they are holding the world's smallest cloud and they cannot let it drop. Make a finish line about 8 to 10 feet away (or have them walk to the far side of the room, turn around, and walk back to the starting line). When you say "go!" they must balance the cotton ball on the spoon and walk to the finish line without letting the cotton ball drop. If it does drop, they must try to pick up the cotton ball with the spoon. This may be challenging for the younger ones, but they will have a good time trying. Play this game indoors.

Cloud hopping—Make a path of clouds for the kids to leap from one cloud to the next. Make the clouds out of poster board or white paper covered with clear contact paper. Since the children will be jumping on them, they need to be durable. The clouds should be placed about a foot and a half away from each other and go all around the rooms of the house.

Another idea for cloud hopping is to give each child two clouds. Tell them that they must go from the starting line to the finish on just those two clouds, so they will need to stand on one while they step to the other and then pick up the one behind them. This is especially fun for the four and five year old kids; younger ones will probably not be able to figure out the process.

Bubbles—Chasing bubbles is always a fun activity for the little folks.

Moon walk—In some cities you can rent a moon walk (a large inflated bubble that the kids jump in) for the day. This can be expensive, but would be a blast for the kids. Check the yellow pages.

Flying—Pretend to fly all over the world. Lead the children in flapping their arms as wings and using their imaginations to pretend they are flying high in the sky. Run around the room or yard as if you are flying. Ask the children to look down and tell everyone what they see. Pretend that you are being blown by the wind or are about to run into a cloud or are holding on to an airplane.

Lay a sheet on the ground to be a cloud. Tell the children that it is time for them all to land on the cloud. Have them gather together and sit down.

Heavenly chorus—Sing some angel songs. Several Christmas songs have angel themes. You can sing them whether it is Christmas time or not. "Angels We Have Heard on High" and "Hark! the Herald Angels Sing" are good choices. Sing the song "Ten Little Indians," substituting the word *angels* for *Indians*.

Sing the tune of "Old McDonald Had a Farm," but use these words:

      God has very special helpers,
        Glory, gloria!

Angels do his special work,
Glory, gloria!
With a _____ , here and a _____ there,
Here a _____ , there a _____ , everywhere a
_____ , _____ .
God has very special helpers,
Glory, gloria!

Fill in the blanks with angel sounds. Think of things that an angel might do. One action would be blowing a horn, so make a *toot* sound by forming your hands like a trumpet at your lips. Another sound would be a *plink, plink* sound from a harp as you strum it. You might make a *flap* sound for the angels wings, or a *clap* to praise the Lord.

If you want to have the children make instruments, they can make a simple horn by taking a paper towel tube and taping a rolled up semi-circle to the end. A harp can be created by taking a shoe box or the lid to the box and putting different sized rubber bands around it. You could also hand out harmonicas or kazoos for the angels to make music. See the Magic Music party in chapter 19 for instrument ideas.

3. Snacks

Gather the children on the cloud and serve them snacks. You can serve the snacks on cloud plates. Glue cotton balls to the edges of white paper plates.

4. Angel talk and craft

When they have finished their snacks, ask the children to remain seated on the cloud. Ask them if they enjoyed being angels and if they think there really are angels. Tell them that the Bible talks about angels often and that there are many stories about God using angels for a special purpose. With older kids, ask if they can remember any stories from the Bible about angels. Read Psalm 91:11 and tell the children that God has angels that watch over us. "Isn't it exciting to think that there are angels that are sent by God to take care of us? Angels are God's helpers."

5. Open presents

While all the children sit on the cloud, let the birthday child sit on a chair so that everyone can see her opening presents. Put a number on each present and put those same numbers in a basket. Let the angels pick out a number and have the birthday child open the corresponding present.

6. Free play

Let the kids play for a while before they go home or provide this fun activity: let the children build marshmallow castles. Set out bowls of large and small marshmallows and let the kids stack them one on top of the other to make castles. They can use glue or toothpicks to hold the marshmallows together. Children can choke easily on marshmallows, so keep a close eye on your guests.

You could also give the children chalk and let them make chalk drawings on blue construction paper.

FOOD:

Serve snacks or just cake and ice cream.

Heavenly fruit salad—Mix mandarin oranges, bananas, and pineapple, together with whipped cream. Serve on a bed of coconut flakes.

Crackers and cheese slices—Cut cheese slices in angel shapes using an angel Christmas cookie cutter.

Ham and bologna trumpets—Roll up slices of meat and secure with a fancy tooth pick.

Angel food cake—Purchase an angel food cake or make your own. Ice it with whipped cream or fluffy egg white icing. Serve with strawberries and ice cream.

FAVORS: Pick and choose

1. Favor bags—Use white lunch sacks for your favor bags. Write the child's name on the sack in gold glitter.
2. Angel costume—halo, white clothing and wings
3. Plastic instrument—trumpet, harmonica or kazoo
4. Small white Frisbee
5. Angel cookie cutters
6. Star or angel stickers
7. Clear plastic frame with clouds painted around the edges. Take polaroid pictures at the party of the little angels or send each child a picture with a thank you note.
8. Bells—Legend says that every time you hear a bell ring, an angel gets his wings.
9. Guardian angel pins are available at most Christian bookstores.
10. Balloons and candy—See if you can find a place that sells bagged cotton candy.

* 6 *

Indian Braves and Princesses Party

Introduce the boys and girls to Native American culture with this fun-filled party. The young braves and princesses will enjoy wearing their colorful feather headbands, playing Indian games and making Indian crafts. The theme, from Joshua 1:9, centers on bravery. "Be strong and of good courage; do not be afraid, nor be dismayed, for the LORD your God is with you wherever you go." You could also combine the Indian theme with a pilgrim theme and focus on giving thanks to the Lord or add some cowboys for a cowboy and Indian theme.

➡ **Suggested Size:**   5 to 12 kids
   Suggested Time of Day: morning or afternoon
   Type: boys, girls, or mixed

YOU WILL NEED:

- Construction Paper
- Feathers
- Plywood
- Fabric
- Coffee cans
- Oatmeal cans

- Milk cartons or shoe boxes
- Poster board
- Yarn and craft sticks
- Toothpicks
- Food

INVITATIONS:

Cut 5-inch triangles out of poster boards and tape three toothpicks at the top of each. Cover the triangles with fabric and cut small flaps to open in the middle. The party information will be written inside the tepees and should read like this:

Chief _____ (child's name) _____ invites
young braves and princesses to pow wow.
Date: _____
Time: _____
Location: _____
RSVP to squaw: _____

DECORATIONS:

You can go wild with the Indian decorations. Make a tepee using three 5-foot plywood boards. Attach them together at the top using rope. Put a bed sheet around the frame or purchase some fabric to staple to the frame. Place the tepee in the backyard or in the main room for the party.

For the front door of your house, make an Indian face out of poster board. Add black construction paper hair and a headband with a feather. Draw the eyes, nose, and mouth. On the headband write the word, *How* or *Welcome*.

Inside your house, place arrows made from poster board or purchase inexpensive toy arrows from the toy store. Hang the arrows on the walls to point the way to the activities. Party colors are red, black, and turquoise. Purchase balloons, streamers, and paper goods in these colors.

Make posters of Indian symbols and drawings. Make "eye of God" crafts to hang around the room. These are made by taking two sticks and securing them with yarn in the center so that they cross to form perpendicular lines. Use different colors of yarn to weave around the sticks. These make lovely decorations. Older kids can make them as a craft at the party.

If you have access to large rolls of paper or fabric, you could make a large triangle tepee to put on the front door. Cut it in the middle for the children to walk through as they enter the party.

SCHEDULE: 1½ hours

15 minutes—Arrive, dress up
10 minutes—Indian games
20 minutes—Indian life
20 minutes—Powwow
10 minutes—Open presents
15 minutes—Free play

ACTIVITIES:

1. Arrive, dress up

Greet each young Indian with a "How" and give him an Indian headband. You can make these headbands a number of different ways depending on the time you want to spend in preparation. The headbands can simply be made out of construction paper and decorated with stickers or drawings. You may choose to make felt headbands with a short piece of elastic in the back. The feather in the back of the headband can be made from construction paper or use real feathers purchased at a craft store.

After presenting your guest with his headband, tell him to follow the arrows to join the rest of the kids. During arrival time, you can have a number of activities for the kids. Pick and choose the activities you want them to do.

Indian vests—Make Indian vests out of brown grocery sacks. Cut a slit up the front of the sack and cut around the bottom of the sack to make the hole for the head. Cut an arm hole on each side and fringe on the edges of the sack. Let the kids decorate and color their vests with markers.

Indian names—Help the children think of Indian names to call themselves. Each child should think of his or her talents and relate them to an animal. They can come up with names such as Running Horse, Fast Deer, or Singing Crow. Write their Indian names on their headbands and vests.

Totem pole—Make a totem pole using boxes or milk cartons. Let the kids decorate their own box, then stack and build to see how high they can make the totem pole.

War paint—Apply Indian war stripes using lipstick and eye pencils.

Bead necklaces—Provide string and beads for the children to make their own Indian bead necklaces.

2. Indian brave games

Direct the children in several running races. Give stickers as prizes to be placed on the vests of everyone who finishes. Give the first place winner a feather for his headband.

The games can be simple races to prove their bravery and speed. Start off with a running race. Then have the kids hop from start to finish. They can race running backwards and then running sideways. You could also make a race in which they somersault or roll to the finish line.

Give the kids a small ball made of crumpled-up foil (the Indians used roots from trees) and kick the ball from start to finish. If you have limited space, have the children go to the end of the room or yard and then back again to the finish line.

Hide and seek—Tell the children that Indians were very good at hiding from their enemies or from animals in the woods. Choose one person to be "It" and let the other children hide. After counting to twenty, the person who is "It" searches for the Indians. When he sees one, he says, "I spy _____." The two race for home base (where the counting was done), then the one who is It goes in search of more Indians. If someone beats the seeker to home base, they get to be the next one to seek.

You can also turn this game around by having one child become the bear, who hides while all of the Indians count to twenty. Then all of the Indians seek the bear. When someone spots the bear, she shouts, "I found the bear," and everyone runs for home base. The first person to touch home base becomes the next bear.

Pony races are another option. Give each Indian a yardstick pony. Make the ponies by using yardsticks for the body and brown or black poster board for the head. Use yarn for the horse's mane and draw on the eye. Attach the poster board to the yardsticks using wood glue or staples and tape. Let them have horse races or just ride around.

3. Indian life

Gather the braves and princesses together in front of the tepee to learn about Indian life. Tell them that Indians loved to dance and sing and that this was an important part of their culture. Give each child a can with construction paper taped around it. Provide markers to let the kids make zigzag designs on the paper covering the can. You can also give them shakers made from small boxes with beans in them.

Tape the edges or use a rubber band to hold the box together. You could also tape two cups together, lip to lip, with beans inside. Lead the children in a rhythm song as they tap and shake to the beat. Make Indian sounds and noises as the kids dance around the tepee.

4. Powwow

Tell the young braves and princesses to all sit Indian style in a circle. Introduce the children to some Indian food, such as beef jerky, corn bread, and berries. Let the kids have a small portion of each. Serve the birthday cake with a tepee and Indian figures on the top.

Use this time to tell the boys and girls that the Indians were very proud of their bravery. Say, "It was a great honor to be considered a brave Indian. What does it mean to be brave? Do you know that the Bible encourages us to be brave with God's strength? Listen as I read what God told Joshua before the Israelites were about to go into the Promised Land."

Read Joshua 1:9. Have the verse written on a colorful poster even if the children cannot read yet. Ask the children if they want to be brave. Tell them to remember that God can give them the courage they need when they are following Him.

5. Open presents

Put all of the presents in the tepee. Tell all of the children to sit in front of the tepee. When you call a name—don't forget to use the Indian name—that child should go into the tepee and come out with his present and give it to the birthday chief.

If this is not a birthday party, you may want to let the children work with some clay or dough to make Indian pottery during this time.

6. Free play

Allow the kids to play with their ponies and bow and arrow sets. You may also want to set out some small plastic cowboy and Indian figures. These small plastic figures would make good favors as well.

FOOD:

Beef jerky—You can find at most grocery stores and convenience stores. Watch small kids with this treat as it may be difficult to chew. Consider using bologna or ham instead for children under four years old.

Corn bread—Prepare your favorite recipe and provide butter, jelly, and honey to go on top.

Berries—Serve berries if they are in season. You might also serve dried fruit.

Punch or juice

Cake—Use your favorite recipe or mix to bake a rectangular cake. Ice the cake with vanilla or chocolate icing. Make several tepees on the top of the cake using ice cream cones with toothpicks sticking out the top. Place some of the plastic Indians on the top of the cake. Make a lake using blue icing. Put a paper canoe in it. On the sides of the cake you can make Indian designs or zigzags in different colors.

FAVORS: Pick and choose from the following:

1. Favor bags—Use brown paper lunch sacks and cut fringe on the top. Make Indian drawings on the sides of the sack.
2. Yardstick ponies—Let the children take home the ponies that they used for the races in activity two.
3. Headbands, feathers, and vests
4. Bow and arrow sets
5. Plastic Indian figures—The figures are available at most toy stores.
6. Balloons
7. Indian beads or jewelry
8. Stone arrowheads—Make some out of clay or purchase them at a museum gift shop.
9. Bowls or cups with Indian designs painted on the side
10. Indian corn—available in the fall, or a small bag of popcorn for children to take home

* 7 *

Wild and Wacky Water Party

Splish, splash, you're going to have a blast at this wonderful water event. All you need is a hose with a sprinkler and an inflatable pool to make this party a splashing success. This is a warm weather event and could go along with a mermaid or boat theme. The kids will wear their bathing suits to play in the water. The story from the Bible will be about Jesus calming the waves in the storm (Mark 4:35–41).

➡ **Suggested Size:**   5 to 15 kids
   Suggested Time of Day: morning or afternoon
   Type: boys, girls, or both

YOU WILL NEED:

- Towels
- Hose and sprinklers
- Squirt bottles
- Inflatable pool or dish-washing tub
- Plastic kitchen items
- Floating ducks and boats
- Balloons and crepe paper streamers
- Food
- Favors
- Fishnet

INVITATIONS:

There are many creative ways to invite your guests to this water party. You can purchase small beach balls and use a permanent marker to write the information on the balls while they are deflated. Mail the deflated beach balls in regular business envelopes. In the catalog listed at the back of this book, you can find small beach balls by the dozen for a very reasonable price. You can also find them at discount stores.

If you want to go a more traditional route, cut a fish or a water drop out of blue poster board and write the party information on the back. You can decorate the fish or water drop with sequins to give it a wet look. Here's what to write:

ITS A WILD AND WACKY WATER PARTY!

_____ is making a
(child's name)

big splash for his [her] _____ birthday.

The water fun starts at _____ and ends at _____ on _____(date)_____ .

Catch the waves at _____
(address)

RSVP _____ .

Please wear your swimsuit.

Rain date _____ .

Give a rain date for about a week after the original date, just in case!

DECORATIONS:

Use blue poster board to cut out large drops of water. On one of the drops write the words _Jesus gives us living water_. Hang drops all around the backyard, on the fence, and on the back porch. You can hang drops from trees or the awning above the back porch. For the front door, draw a large fish on a poster board and write _Welcome_ on bubbles coming from the fish's mouth. You may also want to write instructions about going around to the backyard if you do not want your guests to enter through the front door. Purchase colored fishnets and drape them in several places around the party area.

Your theme colors will be dark blue and light blue. Purchase balloons, streamers, and paper goods in these colors. Hang blue streamers from the tops of the doorways to look like waterfalls. Place blue balloons everywhere, using some helium-filled balloons and some regular balloons. Use only helium balloons if you have children under four years old at the party. If any balloons pop, be sure to pick up the pieces immediately. Don't forget to place some balloons at the mailbox and by the front door.

If you need name tags, make tags shaped as water drops and put each guest's name on a tag before the party. Cover the tag with clear contact paper and pin it to the bathing suit when the guest arrives.

SCHEDULE: 1½ hours

20 minutes—Arrive, sprinkler play
20 minutes—Water games
25 minutes—Snacks
15 minutes—Pool or tub play
10 minutes—Open presents and free play

ACTIVITIES:

1. Arrive, sprinkler play

As children arrive, pin on their name tags and apply sunscreen if they need it. Direct the children to the backyard or another area where the party will take place.

You will want to have the party in an area where you have access to an outdoor faucet. Attach a hose and sprinkler. There are many inexpensive varieties of sprinklers; any one of them will provide fun for the kids. Have the inflatable pool blown up and filled with water for the arriving guests to play in as well. Let the children play, play, play. They need no structure at this point. Let them do their own thing. You may also want to provide balls and bubbles.

WARNING: Do not leave the children unattended for even a minute. Ask several adults to stay and help you watch the children. Assign lifeguard shifts so that the water is being monitored at all times. If you have a built-in swimming pool, do not use it and make sure you have it fenced off from the party. This party is not intended to be a swimming party.

2. Water games

After about twenty minutes of free play, it will be time to play a few games. Here are some suggestions from which to choose.

Hose Hopping—Take the sprinkler off of the end of the hose and tell the children to hop over the stream of water as you hold the hose a few inches off the ground. Next, let them take turns jumping over the water as you make it wiggle like a snake. Make big circles with the hose and let the children try to run through the circles of water.

Squirt fight—Purchase inexpensive squirt or spray bottles from the drug store. Paint the children's names on them if you want to give them away as favors. Give each child a squirt bottle full of water and tell them to squirt each other when you give the signal. One rule: Children can only squirt others from the neck down. If they squirt someone in the face you may want to take away their water bottle for a few minutes.

Duck pond—Put the number 1, 2 or 3 on the bottom of several floating ducks (if you can't find ducks, use boats) and place them in the water. Let each child take a turn to pick a duck. Then have them select a prize from the prize basket that corresponds with the number on the bottom of the duck. The prizes can be small and simple, such as a piece of candy or a whistle or small inflatable toy.

Sponge painting—Provide buckets of water and sponges and let the kids paint pictures on the porch or the driveway or the side of the house. Keep a close eye on the young ones to make sure no one strays into the street from the driveway.

Foam painting—Bring out the foam whipped cream or foam soap and spray designs on your guests. Let an adult be in charge of spraying the foam and try to keep the foam away from the kid's eyes. Let the kids run through the sprinklers to wash clean.

Bubble Up—Pour bubble bath liquid into the pool as you add more water. Let the kids frolic in the bubbles. Hand out bottles of bubbles and let the kids make their own bubbles in the air.

3. Snack time!

Give each child a towel. Use your own towels or make towels out of terry cloth to give to the children as favors. After they have dried off, tell them to sit on their towel so that you can tell them an amazing story about water.

Show the children a picture of Jesus and ask if they know who it is. Tell them that one day Jesus was with His special friends on a boat. "Jesus was in the back of the boat sleeping when a terrible storm came up. Let's all make pretend waves that would be in a big storm." Lead the children to make waves with their arms. You can use a bowl of water and a small toy boat as a visual aid to show the storm and then the calm.

Continue the story:

The disciples became very frightened. They were afraid that their boat would sink. Finally, they woke Jesus and He stood up and spoke to the waves and said, "Peace, be still." Now what do you think happened? You're right! The waves became calm. Jesus' friends were amazed. They said, "Who can this be, that even the wind and the sea obey Him!" We know who He is, don't we? He is Jesus, God's Son. He has the power to calm the stormy sea, and just think what He can do in each of our lives.

After the story, bring out the snacks. Let the kids remain seated and bring their plates to them. When the children get up, gather the towels and hang them out to dry because they will need them again when it is time to leave.

4. Pool play

Tell the kids to come and sit around the outside of the inflatable pool. Put some fun floating toys and kitchen utensils in the pool and allow the children to play. You will want to use items such as funnels, graters, cups, plastic pitchers, and measuring spoons. Use toys such as boats, dolls, and sponge figures as well.

Let the older kids construct their own boats out of foil or Ivory soap, or let them make rafts with craft sticks and glue.

Little girls may enjoy a tub tea party. Let them use a plastic toy tea set to serve tea to their dolls or themselves while sitting in the pool.

5. Open presents and free play

Turn the sprinkler back on and let the kids splash around again, or let them play with the pool toys. Use the last five minutes to dry off and open presents.

FOOD:

Serve up some splashy snacks or simply supply cupcakes and ice cream.

Fish sticks

Blue gelatin—There is now blue gelatin available at your grocery store. Add plain gelatin to make stiffer gelatin squares or fish shapes.

Goldfish snack crackers

Grapes—Cut them in small pieces.

Blue drink mix or punch

Cake and cupcakes—I suggest using a white cake mix and coloring the batter blue. Make any shape cake that you like and ice it with blue icing (white icing colored blue). Use a knife to make waves with the icing. Put boats or mermaids on the top. Make chocolate covered goldfish crackers to go on the sides of the cake; melt chocolate in the microwave, dip the crackers in the chocolate and lay them on wax paper to dry. If you serve cupcakes, put a big glob of icing on the top and use your knife to smooth the icing up to a point to make them look like water drops. You could add chocolate fish on top if you like.

FAVORS: Pick and choose

1. Beach balls—Guests have already received these if you sent them as invitations.
2. Favor sacks can be made from small blue gift bags, with fish or mermaid stickers on the sides.
3. Squirt bottles with guests' names on them.
4. Sunglasses—You can find inexpensive sunglasses at discount stores or drug stores. Paint a small design on the corner of the lens. You may be able to find goggles that are quite inexpensive. Check the catalog suggested in the back.
5. Small bottle of bubbles
6. Duck pond prizes—Give plastic boats, stickers, pencils and other small toys.
7. Small beach towels made out of terry cloth material
8. Decorated visor or flip-flop sandals
9. Balloons and cookies or bubble gum—Give gum to older kids only.
10. Tub toys or soaps molded into special shapes. You may also find finger paint soap and soap crayons.

* 8 *

Circus Celebration

Tricks! Animals! Clowns! Everyone loves the circus! When your guests arrive at the party, they will dress up as clowns and play spectacular circus games. The kids will have a Big Top cake and clown ice cream, then they will gather together to sing happy songs. The biblical theme will teach the children that God wants us to rejoice in Him: "Rejoice in the Lord always" (Philippians 4:4).

➡ **Suggested Size:** 5 to 12 kids
Suggested Time of Day: morning or afternoon
Type: boys, girls, or both

YOU WILL NEED:

- Beach balls
- Poster boards
- Items for carnival games
- Prizes
- Headbands
- Shredded paper
- Glue, tape, paint, markers
- Makeup
- Balloons and crepe paper streamers
- Food and paper goods
- Favors

INVITATIONS:

You will make clown faces for invitations to this party. Cut a 3-inch circle from white poster board to be the clown's face. Cut triangle hats and round red noses from construction paper and put a cotton ball or small pom-pom on the top of the hat. You can make clown hair by gluing red shredded paper (sold in the gift wrap section of most stores) on the sides of the clown head. Draw in diamond-shaped eyebrows and round eyes and a big mouth. On the hat write, *You're invited to a circus celebration*. Write the rest of the party information on the back of the clown face. It should read:

For _____ (child's name) _____ birthday!

Show Time: _____

Big Top Location: _____

RSVP to the Ringmaster: _____

COME TO THE GREATEST PARTY ON EARTH!

DECORATIONS:

Make the party room look like the inside of a circus tent by attaching a variety of colored crepe paper streamers to the center of the ceiling. Distribute the other ends of the streamers at equal intervals around the room. Place plenty of balloons around the room as well.

You will have a multicolor theme, including purple, blue, orange, green, yellow, and red. You may be able to find plates and napkins with clowns printed on them at a party store. If not, choose any of the colors mentioned above and feel free to mix and match them.

Make clown hats for name tags; glue pom-poms on top and print the names vertically on the front. Certain classical melodies make good circus music; "Overture to Paris Life" by Offenbach and "Dance of the Hours" by Ponchielli would be great background music.

For the front door, use a colored poster board and draw a border around the edges. You want this to look like a circus poster. Draw a clown or use circus pictures from magazines to decorate the poster. Write *Welcome to the Big Top!* Attach a few balloons to the front door as well.

SCHEDULE: 1½ hours

20 minutes—Arrive, become a clown

15 minutes—Circus games

20 minutes—Super circus snacks

15 minutes—Happy songs

10 minutes—Open presents
10 minutes—Free play or clown faces

ACTIVITIES:

1. Arrive, become a clown

Dress up as the ringmaster of the circus by wearing a red or black blazer and black pants. Use an eyebrow pencil to draw a fake mustache. You can make a black top hat out of construction paper and a whip from a small stick and string.

As guests arrive, welcome them to the circus and tell them that they should get their clown outfit on because the circus is about to begin. Ask another parent to help in the clown dressing room. If available, use a bedroom with a connecting bathroom to be the clown dressing room. Put a star on the door at the children's eye level that says *Clowns' Dressing Room.*

In the bedroom, the children will receive their clown outfits. For the hats, use cone party hats or black plastic hobo clown hats. Give each child an extra-large boys T-shirt with spots or stripes painted on it. Paint a squiggly line around the neck of the T-shirt to look like a ruffle collar. They will wear the shirts over their own clothes. These could be used as nightshirts for the kids after the party, and will serve as favors and a fun reminder of the event.

Another option is to go to a thrift store and look for any shirts with bright colors or stripes. You may also find some old ties and other fun dress-up clothes for clowns.

Make clown hair by purchasing shredded red paper at a card shop or craft store and attaching it to the sides of a headband. You can buy inexpensive thin plastic headbands by the dozen at any discount store or drug store. I suggest attaching the shredded paper to the headband using tape, glue, or wire trash bag ties. Tape the clown hat to the headband too so that the children have only one object to keep on their heads.

For the clown face, send the kids into the bathroom where another adult will help to apply the makeup. Do not cover the children's faces with white clown makeup. The children will soon become uncomfortable and smudge it. You can use your own makeup or buy face paints or grease crayons at a toy store or party store. Use red lipstick for the nose and mouth and a black eyebrow pencil around the eyes.

After the kids have been transformed into clowns they may want to play around and act like clowns. Let them feel free to go into the main party room to play. Lead them in some tumbling exercises such as somersaults and cartwheels. Put a sheet or a mat down on the carpet to prevent makeup smudges from getting on the carpet and to provide more of a cushion.

2. Circus games

After all the guests have arrived and have had a chance to play a little while, start playing some group games. Choose from the following suggestions.

Obstacle course—An obstacle course is a fun, simple game for little ones. You can make the obstacle course as long and complicated as you want, according to the ages of the children. Here are some obstacle suggestions: crawl under a table, stand on a chair, jump over a jump rope, walk through a hoop, climb into a laundry basket, do a cartwheel, crawl under a rope, run around plastic cones.

Bubbles—Blow bubbles and let the clowns try to pop them. Give the children a chance to blow bubbles too.

Play Ball—Using an inflated beach ball, let the kids toss the ball back and forth to each other as they stand in a circle. You can also let them roll or kick the ball to each other. Use a bed sheet to bounce the ball as everyone holds onto the sides of the sheet.

Circus Animals—Let the kids pretend to be animals at the circus. Ask the kids what kinds of animals they see at the circus. When they say an animal, tell everyone to act like that animal. Here are some possibilities: dancing bears, dogs doing tricks, show elephants, tamed lions.

Carnival games—You will need some parents to help you with this activity. You will also need quite a few small prizes. Let the kids do the games together as a whole group, or if you have more than eight kids, split them into groups and let them play the different games one group at a time. Each child gets a prize for trying. Give the kids their favor bags to hold the prizes. Here are some suggested games:

- Bean bag toss
- Throw the ball into the laundry basket
- Hidden prizes in a tub of rice
- Pick a lollipop—Stick lollipops in a foam square or in the bottom of a shoe box. Each lollipop has a color on the bottom of

the stick. The child gets to choose a prize from the basket with the corresponding color.

- Toss a penny in the circle
- Putt a golf ball into a can
- Throw a hoop over stuffed animals

3. Snack time!

Cut large stars out of colored poster boards and lay them on the floor in a circle. Let each child sit on a star to eat his circus lunch.

4. Happy songs

As the children finish their snacks, encourage them to sit on their stars. Say:

Isn't it fun to laugh? Do you think God wants us to laugh? Many, many verses in the Bible tell us to be glad and rejoice! It is fun to be a clown because we wear a painted smile, but God wants us to wear a real smile. When we have God in our lives, He gives us joy.

Read Philippians 4:4.
If you know the song "Rejoice in the Lord Always," sing it with the children. Lead the children in some other simple happy songs. You do not need to be a good singer to do this. Here are some suggestions:

- "If You're Happy and You Know It"
- "I've Got That Joy, Joy, Joy, Joy Down in My Heart"
- "Ho, Ho, Ho, Hosanna, Ha, Ha, Hallelujah"
- "Ha Lel La Lel La Lel La Lel Lu Jah"
- "Rejoice in the Lord Always"

If you do not know how to sing these songs, ask your children's choir director or youth minister or someone that you know who may be familiar with youth songs. If you are at a loss in leading the singing, use your tape recorder to tape someone who can sing the songs or invite that person to the party. You can also look at your Christian bookstore to see what kind of fun kids tapes they may carry.

Do not expect the children to sit and sing all the songs. Stand up for some songs, clap and skip to some of the songs and only sing as many songs as they seem to be able to handle.

5. Open presents

After you finish singing, tell the kids that it is time for the birthday child to open presents. Let the birthday child take center stage by sitting on a chair while everyone else remains seated on their star. Dim the lights and shine a flashlight on the child opening the presents.

6. Free play or clown faces

If you have smaller children at the party, I suggest some free play at this time. If you are looking for one more structured activity, you can let the children make clown faces with construction paper. Pre-cut colored shapes and figures and let the children glue them on the clown faces. You will want to cut red circles for the noses, black triangles for the eyes, and a big red smile for the mouth. You can add a hat and hair as well.

Gumdrop art is another fun activity. Provide a wide assortment of gumdrops, glue, and paper. Let the kids create pictures and scenes with the gumdrops.

FOOD:

Hot dogs—Slice in half lengthwise.

Pretzels

Clown lips—Take two apple slices and spread peanut butter on one side of each. Put miniature marshmallows on the peanut butter side of one slice and put the other slice down over the marshmallows. Now you have a mouth with funny marshmallow teeth.

Juice or punch

Big Top cake—Use your favorite cake recipe to make a round layer cake. Use white icing and multicolored sparkles on the top and sides. Make pennant flags using tooth picks and tissue paper to decorate the top of the cake.

Clown ice cream—A famous old idea! Put a scoop of ice cream in a dish and use an ice cream cone for a clown hat. Decorate with raisins for the eyes and red licorice for the nose and mouth. Use shredded coconut for the hair. You can also use decorative icing to make the clown's features. You may want to use this clown creation instead of cake as the dessert.

FAVORS: Pick and choose

1. Favor bags—Provide white lunch sacks with multicolored dots drawn on them.
2. Clown nightshirts, hair headbands and hats
3. Horns or noise makers

4. Box of animal crackers
5. Plastic circus animals
6. Plastic or rubber balls
7. Prizes from carnival games
8. Large funny glasses
9. Circus posters featuring a Polaroid picture of the guests
10. Small paperback books or coloring books about the circus

∗ 9 ∗

Prince and Princess Party

Your little prince or princess will have a royal time at this enchanted celebration. The guests will dress up as royalty and enjoy imperial games and a magnificent feast. A puppet show teaches the children about Esther, a true princess from the Bible who saved her people from harm.

➡ **Suggested Size:**   5 to 12 kids
    Suggested Time of Day: morning or afternoon
    Type: boys, girls, or both

YOU WILL NEED:

- Parchment paper
- Yellow and white poster boards
- Yardsticks
- Construction paper
- Dress-up clothes
- Purple netting
- Balloons
- Dolls for puppets
- Food

INVITATIONS:

Make invitations from parchment paper so that they look like royal proclamations. Write the party information on 5-inch by 7-inch parchment paper, available at craft stores. Use calligraphy or nice handwriting, or type the invitation. The information should read as follows:

The Honor of Your Presence
is requested at a Royal Ball
to honor Princess _____ (child's name)
on the occasion of her _____th birthday.
Royal hour: _____
Palace address:_____

(Optional)   A Royal Feast will be served.

RSVP Queen _____ (mother's name)

Roll up the invitation and tie it with a purple ribbon. Hand deliver the invitations or buy small mailing tubes at a local mail packaging store. You could also fold the invitation flat and mail it in a regular envelope.

DECORATIONS:

The theme is centered around the medieval period, with the theme colors purple and gold. Write the words, *Welcome to* _____'s *Castle,* on a poster board and cover the letters with glitter. Tape or staple fringe trim to the bottom of the poster. Attach the poster somewhere near the front door.

Let the children enter through a drawbridge into the castle. There are several ways you can create this effect. Locate a large packing box from any store that sells appliances or televisions. Paint the box gray and cut squares out of the roof to resemble the top of a castle. Put four purple triangle flags on sticks at the corners. Cut a rectangle door that opens by pulling down like a drawbridge. Attach ropes from the corners of the drawbridge to the castle. Cut a hole in the back of the castle so that the kids can walk through the castle as they arrive. This will be an exciting and fun entrance for them.

Put purple and gold balloons throughout the party rooms, and use them to decorate the mailbox too. Use colored poster boards to make decorative crowns and shields to hang on the walls. Label the different party rooms in the house as follows: *Royal Kitchen, Royal Bathroom, Royal Playroom,* etc. The plates and napkins can be purple or white. Use plastic goblets for drinks. This is best for four and five year olds who are less likely to spill. Make name tags from colored construction paper in the shape of jewels.

SCHEDULE: 1½ hours

15 minutes—Arrive, decorate crowns
15 minutes—Dress up
15 minutes—Horse races
20 minutes—Royal feast
15 minutes—Puppet show
10 minutes—Royal gifts and favors

ACTIVITIES:

1. Arrive, decorate crowns

As the children arrive, welcome them to the Royal Land of Birthday Fun. Give the children their name tags and direct them to the room where they can decorate their crowns. Give the boys regular circular crowns, and give the girls cone-shaped crowns with purple netting attached to the top.

To make the girls' crowns, cut yellow poster board in the shape of a half circle. Roll the poster board so that the straight edge is at the top of the cone and the rounded part is at the base. Tape the ends together and attach the netting to the top of the girls' cones. Then staple elastic to go under their chins.

Provide markers, sequins, and decorative stickers for the kids to decorate their crowns. Use glue sticks or apply regular glue with cotton swabs to attach the sequins.

Provide beads to string and pictures to color for those who finish early. For active children who are not craft oriented, provide blocks or boxes so that they can build castles of their own. Or let the kids continue to play at the drawbridge if they want.

2. Dress up

Several weeks before the party, begin collecting old clothes from your own closet and from thrift stores. I found one thrift store that had a special sale that allowed me to fill an entire grocery sack with clothes for a few dollars. I stuffed the bag full of frilly chiffons and other clothes with silky fabrics. I also found blazers and vests.

Boys may like capes and royal robes. They can make swords or shields from poster boards as part of their costumes too. The girls will probably enjoy long, flowing dresses. Old nightgowns and bridesmaid dresses work well. You can add jewelry for the girls to wear and a little makeup, too, if you like. Take pictures of the kids in their costumes. If you use a Polaroid camera, you can give the pictures as favors.

After the children have tried on several outfits, let them play the royal jewel game. To play this game, choose one person to be the prince to guard over the jewel placed at his feet. The jewel can be a piece of jewelry, a crown, or anything easy to pick up. The rest of the children stand around the prince in a circle and try to take the jewel. The prince must keep the children away by trying to tag them. If they are tagged, they must go back and sit at the edge of the circle. When someone gets the jewel, he or she becomes the new prince.

3. Royal horses

Give each child a yardstick horse to ride. You will make these ponies before the party, using yardsticks (usually free from hardware stores) and poster board horse heads. Cut two horse heads for each horse. Attach black yarn for the horse's mane. Staple and tape the heads to the yardsticks. Use brown poster boards for the heads, or paint white poster boards, brown. These ponies make wonderful party favors. As you give each child their horse, tell her to think of a name for the horse. Let everyone tell the group the name that she has chosen.

Lead the royal guests in some circle activities with the horses. Tell the riders to circle to the left and then to the right; then have them go to the center of the circle and then back again. Try other horse stunts like turning around, prancing, and jumping. Then let the horses gallop around the room. You may want to set up a race or an obstacle course for them to follow. Let them enjoy some free play with the horses as well.

Here are some suggestions for more games if you have extra time.

Hidden treasures—Use a big box or plastic baby pool and fill with shredded newspaper. Tell the children that they must find a jewel hidden in the hay. Hide candy or small prizes in the shredded paper. Tell the children that they are each supposed to find one prize.

Musical crown—You will need one special crown and several chairs for this game. Make one chair a throne by draping a blanket or velvet fabric over it. Let the children sit on the chairs, set in a circle. Play royal-sounding music and tell them to stand up and begin walking around the circle. When the music stops, the children are to sit down. The child who ends up sitting on the throne gets to wear the extra-special crown for the next round until there is a new winner.

Drop the crown—Use the same special crown to play this game. Sit the children in a circle on the floor and let one child start as the king. The king walks around the outside of the circle and drops the crown behind someone's back. That person must stand up and put on the crown and chase the king back to the empty spot in the circle. The new king proceeds in the same manner.

4. Royal feast

Invite the children into the banquet hall where they will enjoy a royal feast, or you may choose simply to serve cake and ice cream. If possible, try to have a small banquet table for the children. You could use coffee tables covered in plastic tablecloths or children's tables. If you do not have enough chairs, the kids can sit on the floor and still eat comfortably.

5. Puppet show

After the kids have finished eating, gather them into the den for a puppet show. Use fashion dolls like Barbie or other dolls for the show. You will need one doll to represent Queen Esther, one for King Ahasuerus and one for Haman. Tell the following story from the book of Esther using the figures to act the story out as you speak. You do not need to be behind a curtain, although you could ask another adult to help hold up the dolls as you tell the story:

The Bible tells us that once there was a beautiful maiden named Esther who was one of God's chosen people, an Israelite. When the king in the land decided to choose a wife, he picked Esther above all the other women because of her beauty. It was a beauty that God had given her, beauty that came from the inside out.

One day a bad man named Haman decided that all of the Israelites must be killed. Esther was very upset because this meant that all of her people, including her, would be put to death.

God had a purpose and a plan for Queen Esther. Esther bravely went to the king. It was a brave thing to do because anyone who approached the king without an invitation could be killed if the king so desired. But God was with Esther, and the king welcomed her. Esther was very wise and invited both the king and Haman to dinner. After a second night at dinner, Esther told the king about Haman's plan to kill the Israelites. She asked the king for help. The king loved Esther and granted her request and also had the bad man, Haman, killed.

If the kids are older, tell more of the details of the story. You may also want to mention to the older children that God has sent a Prince to save us from death as well. Tell them that Jesus is the Prince of

Peace and He died on the cross and rose again so that all who believe in Him would not die but have eternal life.

6. Royal gifts

Let the birthday child sit on the throne as the guests sit on the floor holding their presents. Stand next to the throne and use a pretend scroll to call out the children's names one at a time: "Princess _____ will now present her gift."

FOOD:

Provide a royal feast or serve just dessert.

Meat—Serve slices of bologna and ham.
Rolls—Most children love rolls or biscuits of any kind.
Fruit—Kids will enjoy grapes, apple slices, and orange slices.
Cheese—Slice any kind.
Lemonade or punch—Serve in small plastic goblets.
Castle cake—Using your favorite cake recipe or mix, bake two cakes in bread pans. Use one cake as the main building of the castle and cut the other cake into four pieces to be the towers. Place the cake in the freezer over night so that it will be sturdy when you are ready to ice it. Ice the entire castle in chocolate icing. Put small flags made out of toothpicks on the tops of the towers. You could also use ice cream cones as the towers. Another cake idea is to bake a round cake and put a plastic or cardboard crown on top.

FAVORS: Pick and choose

1. Yardstick ponies
2. Crowns
3. Beaded necklaces—Do not give these to smaller children.
4. Prizes—Kids will keep what they find in the hidden treasures game.
5. Pouches with candy money—Make small pouches using purple tissue paper or fabric. Place chocolate candy coins in the center and tie the pouch with gold ribbon.
6. Plastic jewelry
7. Gold stickers
8. Decorated plastic boxes—Purchase small, inexpensive plastic

boxes used for knickknacks. Decorate with paint or stickers and call them treasure boxes.

9. Gold painted frame for the Polaroid pictures taken at dress-up

10. Royal scepters—Make these from a baton or make glittered covered sticks with a ball or a star at the end.

* 10 *

Camp Jubilee

Invite the kids to camp out in your own backyard at Camp Jubilee. The children will pack their knapsacks and take an exciting hike that will lead them to the campsite. Campers will sing camp songs and tell stories around a pretend fire. The biblical theme is that all creation worships God. Psalm 96:11–12 says, "Let the heavens rejoice, and let the earth be glad;/Let the sea roar, and all its fullness;/Let the field be joyful, and all that is in it./Then all the trees of the woods will rejoice before the Lord."

⇒ **Suggested Size:**   5 to 15 kids
  Suggested Time of Day: morning or afternoon
  Type: boys, girls, or mixed

YOU WILL NEED:

- Camping gear
- Tent
- Branches and twigs
- Construction paper
- Plastic bags
- Grocery bags
- Toilet paper rolls

- Colored tape
- Hangers
- Netting
- Dowel rods or sticks
- Note cards or poster board

INVITATIONS:

Write the party information on a plain white note card or a 3-inch by 5-inch piece of poster board. Decorate the card with a simple drawing of a pine tree and a tent.

The party information should read as follows:

```
Join us at Camp Jubilee
for _____ Birthday!
            (child's name)
Camp hours: _____ to _____
Camp date: _____
Camp location: _____
Let the camp director know that you are coming;
Call _____ .
```

You can send the card as it is; or make it more interesting by attaching it to a pine cone, whistle, or cap and hand deliver them all.

DECORATIONS:

Weather permitting, this party would be best outdoors, but will work just fine indoors. Wherever you are, you can decorate with streamers and balloons. You will be working with camouflage colors such as green, brown, and gray. Purchase green balloons, streamers, and paper goods.

Set up a tent in your backyard. If you do not own one, borrow one from a friend or make your own using poles and bed sheets.

On the front door, make a welcome sign using brown poster board. Use a black marker to make the poster look like burned wood. Color a white poster brown if you cannot find brown poster board. Write the words *Welcome to Camp Jubilee.*

Make another sign on green poster board, writing the theme Bible verses on it. After you have written the words on the poster, glue or tape leaves to the outer rim of the poster.

If your party is indoors, bring in some branches or make some fake branches with leaves to set around the room. Make name tags from construction paper in the shape of leaves or pine trees.

SCHEDULE: 1½ hours

15 minutes—Arrive, backpack, decorate caps or visors
30 minutes—Hike and games
20 minutes—Chow down
10 minutes—Camp songs, talk
15 minutes—Open presents and free play

ACTIVITIES:

1. Arrive, backpack, decorate caps or visors

Wear a sweatshirt with letters taped or painted on the front to say *Camp Jubilee* and put a whistle around your neck so that you look like a camp counselor. As the campers arrive, pin on their name tags and tell them to join the other campers as they prepare their backpacks.

There are several different options for the backpack. My favorite idea is to make backpacks out of brown paper grocery sacks. Cut away the top half of the front and sides of the bag. The top of the back will act as a flap to close the backpack. Attach velcro strips to serve as a latch to make the flap stay closed.

Use the paper that was cut off to make the backpack's straps. Cut the piece into two equal strips and fold the paper in half twice to make the straps sturdy; then attach them to the pack using staples and strong tape. You could also use thick ribbon or material for the straps. It is most important to make sure that the straps are secure so that they do not break, or you will have some unhappy campers. These backpacks are easy to make and inexpensive, and the kids love them!

Another option is to sew a simple backpack using camouflage or green heavy cotton fabric. If you have a small group of guests, you may consider buying inexpensive backpacks.

As you greet guests at the door, let another adult help the children fill their backpacks. Provide several different items to pack. Choose from these selections:

Trail mix—Let the kids fill a plastic bag with trail mix (dry cereal, raisins, pretzels, M&Ms) and a juice drink box.

Compass—Children will need their pretend compasses to help them on their hike. Cut round circles from poster board and write *N, S, E,* and *W* on them. Stick brads through the centers and fold them to one side to act as the needles of the compasses.

Whistle—You can find inexpensive plastic whistles at discount stores.

Binoculars and/or a magnifying glass—Make binoculars by taping two
toilet paper rolls together side by side using black tape. You can also
cover the rolls with black construction paper. The binoculars will be
fun to have on the hike as the children look for special birds. They
may also like to have a small plastic magnifying glass to observe some
parts of nature close up.

Butterfly net—You can make a simple butterfly net by attaching inexpensive netting to a hanger. Straighten the hanger, and then bend it
into a circle at one end to attach the netting. Straighten the hanger's
hook to make the handle for the net. Use colored tape to cover the
handle. Do not use with children 3 or under.

Other items to consider for the backpack, if you want to spend the
money, are small flashlights, plastic canteens, and sunglasses. When
the kids finish packing their backpacks, let them decorate the
backpacks with stickers.

Do leaf rubbings with children who finish early. Leaf rubbings are
made by simply taking a leaf and putting a piece of thin paper over it.
Use the side of a crayon on paper over the leaf. An impression of the
leaf will show up on the paper.

You can also give the campers a cap or visor. Make your own visors
by cutting a semicircle from thick construction paper and attaching
string or elastic from one end to the other. Let the kids decorate their
visors too. As an extra, you could also give each child a T-shirt with
Camp Jubilee printed or painted on it.

2. Hike and camp games

Gather the campers together and tell them that they are going to
take a hike to the campsite. During the hike, they can be on the
lookout for butterflies, birds, and animals. Tell them to be sure to
follow their counselor.

If you have nice weather, you will want to take the kids outside for
the hike. Decide before the party the path that you want to take. You
can take a short walk around the neighborhood if the kids are older. If
they are younger, hike around your yard. You can also hike inside the
house through every room. If you have stairs, the kids can pretend
that they are mountain climbing.

Set up certain activities along the hike route. For instance, make
simple tissue paper butterflies by cutting out several tissue paper
rectangles and gathering them in the middle with a pipe cleaner. Hang
the butterflies from a tree on the hike route or from the ceiling in one
of your rooms using thread. Let the kids try to catch the butterflies
with their nets. Make at least one butterfly per child. If they are hung

by thread, you will need to break the thread when the child has caught his butterfly. Tell them to put their butterflies in their backpacks.

Another idea is to draw animal tracks on the sidewalk or use index cards with tracks drawn on them and taped to the floor. Make several different kinds of tracks and ask the kids if they can guess what kind of animal made the tracks. Ask them to look around to see if they find any of these animals. Before the party, hide a stuffed animal or a picture of an animal. See if the children can find it. Gather everyone back to the hiking trail and keep moving.

Look for birds. Tell the kids to get out their binoculars and look for different types of birds. If you are outside, you can look for actual birds. If you are inside, use pictures hung around the room. Ask the kids if they can find the red bird or the blue bird or the biggest bird. After observing birds, resume your hike.

At a good stopping point, tell the campers that it is time to sit and rest. Tell them to get their snacks out of their backpacks and let them enjoy their trail mix and juice. Talk about how much fun it is to go hiking and tell them that they will be getting to the campsite soon. When they finish, use a trash bag to collect all of the trash.

As you are about to continue along your way, tell the children to get their compasses out of their bags. Ask them if they know what a compass is and how to use it. Tell them it is a device to help you determine which direction you are going. Explain that compasses have special needles that always point north, so you can figure out what direction you are going. Point out the different letters on the compass and tell the children what they stand for; then continue your hike.

3. Chow down

Lead the children back to your yard or to a room where you have set up the tent. Tell the kids to take off their backpacks and start looking for firewood for the campfire. Before the party, scatter twigs and small branches near the tent for the kids to gather. If the party is indoors, you can use rolled up brown construction paper for branches and twigs. Whether you are inside or outside, make a fake fire using orange, red, and yellow construction paper or tissue paper.

Bring out cake and ice cream to eat around the campfire. See the food section for details.

4. Camp songs, talk

As the campers are finishing their refreshments, ask them if they enjoy being out in nature and in God's wonderful creation. Tell the kids that the Bible says that even the fields and the trees praise God.

Show the poster with the theme verses written on it and read it to them. Ask the kids, "If the fields and the trees praise Him, shouldn't we praise Him too?" Sing around the campfire. If you need help leading the singing, ask a friend or youth leader to help. You can use a tape recorder too. I suggest the *Wee Sing Bible* and/or *Camp* tapes and the *Psalty Sing Along* tapes.

Telling stories is another fun event around the campfire. Ask the kids if they know any Bible stories that they want to tell. Help them out if they get stuck, but give them an opportunity to tell it the best they can. If no one seems to remember a Bible story, help them get started by saying something like, "I remember a story about a giant and a little boy. Does anyone remember that story?"

Keep this time reasonably short and observe the attention span of the children. If they seem to want to get up and run around, skip the storytelling time or limit it to one or two stories.

5. Open presents

Place all of the presents in the tent. Let the campers sit around the campfire in a circle with the birthday child sitting on a chair. When you call out a camper's name, that camper will go get his present from the tent and give it to the birthday child. You will want one adult in the tent helping the campers to find their presents. If this is not a birthday party, lead the kids in a game of leap frog. Allow the children to have some free play time at the end of the party so they can play in the tent or play with their backpacks.

FOOD:

The kids will have trail mix and juice on the hike, but if you want to serve them lunch around the campfire, here are a few suggestions.

Grilled hot dogs—Cut hotdogs lengthwise.
Apples or orange slices
Chips or crackers
Punch or juice
Ladybug Cupcakes—Bake your favorite cupcakes and ice them with red-orange icing (white icing mixed with food coloring). Use raisins to make the spots on the back of the ladybug. Shoe string licorice makes good wings. If you want to have a big cake, make a round cake using this same idea. Or if you have a Christmas tree cake pan, you could make a pine tree cake.
S'mores—If you choose to make the familiar camp dessert called *S'mores*, you will need graham crackers, miniature marshmallows,

and chocolate bars. On one graham cracker, put marshmallows and on another put a chocolate bar. Place on a cookie sheet and broil for about a minute. The chocolate should be slightly soft and the marshmallows should be slightly brown. Take them out and put the two sides together. Allow the dessert to cool before giving it to the campers. This treat received it's name from the fact that they taste so good everyone wants some more!

WARNING: S'mores are extremely messy. You will need a good supply of wet paper towels on hand. Don't serve them for two and three year olds. For others, serve the treat outside, if possible.

FAVORS:

There is no need for any more favors because the children have their backpacks filled with goodies. You may want to give a balloon and some candy to the children as they leave.

Ages Six Through Nine

Six and nine year olds are about as much alike as apples and oranges. Both fruits, but with vastly different characteristics. Many changes take place between these ages, so this section covers a wide range of development. Children grow more independent, expressive, and opinionated through these years. Generally the children are nice and sweet, but as they get older, they begin to have their moments of unkindness.

Strong friendships develop among children in this age group, and along with these friendships come cliques and clubs. Be especially sensitive when you are dividing into groups or choosing partners. Children can easily hurt other children's feelings, and you do not want to see this happen at a party. In each party, I have suggested ways to divide into groups or couples for the games so that the choosing is done randomly, not by choosing favorites.

Children in this age group like to be entertained. Many of the kids are accustomed to watching TV and playing video games, so parties must be full of activities to keep their interest. The parties in this section are loaded with activities and games to play. Pick and choose the ones that you want to use. It is better to have too many activities to fill the time than too few.

It is best to keep the parties given for this age group limited to all boys or all girls. The kids seem more comfortable with this arrangement. Girls tend to be slightly more inhibited when they are around boys. If there are no boys present, then girls are more active and talkative. Boys can be confident, rowdy and full of energy at this age. Girls will cooperate easily with most games and activities, whereas boys tend to be skeptical. You will generally find that boys will complain before they actually know the whole story, so just remain positive and encourage the boys to participate anyway. Once they are actually doing an activity, they usually become enthusiastic and play very well together.

I suggest inviting between five and fifteen guests. If you invite more than fifteen children, you can break the activities into small groups, but be sure you have several adult helpers whom you have instructed beforehand as to what they need to do.

Invitations are less cutesy but still creative and intriguing. Decorations should be colorful and set the mood for the party. Favors may cost a little more for this age group. Remember that the favor list is long, so just choose a few items to give to the kids. Let your child help make invitations and choose decorations and favors.

This is a very creative time in the children's lives. They are able to draw and build with greater skill, and their imaginations are still very vivid. Crafts are popular, so you will see that most of the parties involve imaginative crafts to take advantage of the talents beginning to flow.

Six year olds are still young and may need help on certain crafts and games. Many of them cannot read very well yet, so draw pictures instead of words. This is still a tender age, and they may not be overly confident with games. Be sensitive to their confidence level, especially if there are older kids present.

Seven and eight year olds participate well and enjoy learning, yet they become bored easily, so keep the activities moving. Some of the kids may want to rush through crafts and games, so encourage them to take their time and do their best. At these ages, children are growing in confidence and maturity. They are able to do a lot more on their own and are proud of the fact that they do not need your help quite as much.

By the time children reach age nine, they feel as if they know almost as much as you do, if not more. They are also beginning to care deeply about what their friends think. Their parties are important to them, and they will want to impress others with what they do. Let your son or daughter play a big part in the decisions about the party. Some kids may feel some of the parties are too young for them. This is a transition age, so consider the parties in the next section as well.

Remind your child that these parties are a way to minister to others. Kids in this age group can begin to think of other people's needs instead of just their own. Be sure to encourage this quality in them. Party on!

* 11 *

Fabulous Flowers

Let's get back to nature! Girls will enjoy planting their own garden and going on a nature walk. Decorated visors, pinwheels, and vegetable art will all be part of the fun. Snacks will include flower sandwiches and an ice cream dessert in a flower pot. The biblical theme comes from John 15:5: "I am the vine, you are the branches."

➡ **Suggested Size:**   5 to 15 kids
  Suggested Time of Day: morning or afternoon
  Type: girls

Note: I recommend this party for the spring, summer or early fall. A good alternative location for this party would be a large park or local arboretum.

YOU WILL NEED:

- Construction paper
- Artificial flowers
- Seeds and dirt
- Foil trays
- Dowel rods and tacks
- Balloons and crepe paper streamers
- Visors and decorations
- Poster boards
- Whistle
- List of nature items and bag

INVITATIONS:

Make invitations shaped like a flower in a flower pot. Use brown poster board (or white poster board colored brown) and cut it out in the shape of a flower pot three inches high and about two inches wide. You will write most of the party information on the pot as you see below.

You're Invited to a Fantastic Flower Party!

Date: _____

Time: _____

Place: _____

RSVP: _____

Use green pipe cleaner for the flower's stem, or if you can't find pipe cleaners, use green construction paper. Using bright pink and yellow paper, cut out flower shapes and cut a small hole in the middle to pull the pipe cleaner through and then knot the pipe cleaner. Tape the other end of the pipe cleaner to the back of the brown flower pot. On the flower write the initial greeting, "It's (child's name)'s Birthday!"

Another idea for invitations is to write the party information on a note and attach it to an artificial flower and hand deliver it or put it in an envelope to mail. You can purchase a group of six artificial flowers at a discount store for a small cost.

DECORATIONS:

Use the colors pink and yellow for balloons and streamers to decorate the party room. Using large yellow and pink poster boards, cut shapes of flowers and hang them all around the room. Copy John 15:5 on one of the flowers. Write *Welcome* on another flower to be taped to the front door. As a centerpiece for the refreshment table, you may want to use a live flower arrangement, or put some carnations in a vase and at the end of the party use the carnations as favors for your guests.

Buy plates, cups, and napkins in solid colors to match the balloons and streamers, or use paper goods with a floral design. If you need name tags, tape or glue small artificial flowers to plain white name tags.

SCHEDULE: 2 hours

20 minutes—Arrive, decorate visors, vegetable art
40 minutes—Nature walk or indoor games
30 minutes—Time to eat
30 minutes—Plant garden, open presents

ACTIVITIES:

1. Arrive, decorate visors, vegetable art

Greet guests at the door with a smile, give them their name tags, and show them where they can decorate their visors. Purchase bright colored visors at a craft store or make your own from poster board and elastic. Cut the visor shade, then staple a 10-inch piece of elastic ($\frac{1}{2}$- or $\frac{3}{4}$-inch wide) to the ends.

Provide stickers, paint, glitter, glue, and ribbons for decorating the visors. Encourage the girls to take their time and to use their imaginations to make beautiful and unique creations.

Some girls will finish sooner than others, so it is always good to have a second project to do. A fun art project is to make ink stamps out of vegetables. Use potatoes, carrots, and radishes as stamps. Simply cut a vegetable in half and cut the flat side to form a design that stands out. Dip the vegetable stamp into tempera paint, then imprint on either cloth or paper. You may want to use this project to have the girls decorate their favor bags after they have had a chance to practice on paper.

2. Nature walk or indoor games

If you have nice weather, take the girls on a nature walk in your neighborhood or at a nearby park. There are many benefits and joys to be found in a walk through nature. Even if you walk in your own neighborhood, there are lots of things to observe that we rarely notice in our busy lives.

Before you begin your walk, divide the girls into groups of three or four girls each. Before the party, take several different colors of construction paper and cut out three or four leaves in each color. Put the leaves in a bag. Divide into groups by asking each guest to pull a leaf out of the bag. She will join the others who have leaves of the same color.

As the groups form you will give each group a list of items to look for. This is a nature scavenger hunt. You can have the girls hunt in your yard before the walk or search for items during the walk. Give each group a bag to hold its collection. Your list can include items such as ladybugs, wild flowers, three different shapes of leaves, pine cones, four different colored rocks, tall grass, worms, acorns, dandelions, feathers, three sticks of different lengths. Draw pictures of the items if the girls are young and cannot read yet. Set some guidelines for the hunt. I suggest:

- Each group must stay together.
- Each group must stay where you can see them.
- Each group has exactly twenty minutes.
- Girls must not pick flowers or special items from other people's yards.
- When you blow the whistle, the teams have thirty seconds to join you.

When the scavenger hunt is over, count to see which group has the most items from the list. Give the girls in that group a small prize such as a package of stickers or a note pad with flowers on it.

For the next activity, hand each girl several pieces of white paper and a crayon. Tell the girls to use the side of their crayon to make rubbings. Have them hold their paper against the side of a tree and rub the paper with their crayon. The pattern from the bark will make a unique design. Ask them to try several different types of trees and notice the different designs that are formed.

You can also consider bird watching or planting a new tree as a group.

After these activities, gather the entire group to one tree. Have them sit down on a large quilt or blanket. If you anticipate any mud, bring plastic trash bags to put under the quilt. Begin your talk by holding up a dead branch from a tree. Ask the children if the branch could bud or have leaves. Ask them why it couldn't. Help lead them to the conclusion that it must be attached to the tree. Read John 15:5. Then say, "Jesus says that we need to be attached to Him just like a branch is attached to the tree. We need to abide in Christ, but how do we do that?" Let them answer.

Talk about bearing fruit:

Jesus says if we abide in Him, we will bear much fruit. Does that mean we are going to start sprouting apples and oranges? What is the fruit He is talking about? The Bible talks about several different kinds of fruits. Here are the fruits of the Spirit listed in Galatians 5:22–23: love, joy, peace, longsuffering, kindness, goodness, faithfulness, gentleness, and self-control. I know that I would like to have these fruits in my life, what about you?

Let's try to be fruitful branches and not dead sticks!

After your talk, head back home for snacks or have a picnic where you are.

The following are some suggestions for indoor fun, in case of bad weather. Break into groups of about three or four girls using the method suggested at the beginning of the nature walk.

Flower Power—Give each group a poster board and a basket full of cut-out paper flowers. The flowers should be all different colors, shapes, and sizes. The groups will be given five minutes to produce pictures using all of the flowers in their baskets. Make sure each group has an equal number of flowers. The pictures they produce can be any scene that they choose: a house, a farm scene, downtown buildings, mountains, etc. After each group finishes, they will hold up their pictures while the rest of the groups try to guess what it is. You may want to give prizes for creativity, best use of flowers, and uniqueness.

Nature acting—Call out an object found in nature and have everyone act like that object. Here are some fun objects to try: a cloud, a blade of grass, a leaf falling from a tree, a caterpillar, or a fly. You can go on for quite a while with this game. Let the girls come up with some ideas on their own.

Pretend nature walk—Lead the kids on a nature walk inside the house. Pretend you are crossing the creek, climbing a mountain (your stairs), and bird watching (looking out the window). Use your imagination as you lead the kids along the walk.

Flower necklaces—Sit on the floor in a circle with the materials the girls need to make the necklaces in the center. For the flower necklaces, use the same pattern for the flower that you made for the invitation, minus the pot and stem. You will precut about 10 to 15 paper flowers for each guest. Have your daughter help you with this task. It should go fairly fast since you can cut out three or four flowers at one time. Provide also for each guest a 30-inch piece of string or yarn with one end knotted. The girls will make their necklaces by stringing the flowers through the center and adding beads in between the flowers. You can purchase beads at a craft store or make your own using painted uncooked macaroni or colored drinking straws cut into small pieces. Encourage the girls to create their own designs and patterns. As they finish, help them tie the ends together.

Make pinwheels—Using bright colored paper, markers, stickers, and glitter, make unique and creative pinwheels. Cut a 5-inch paper square diagonally from each corner but leave the center intact. You now have eight corners; pull every other one to the center. Be careful not to crease the paper. Push a tack through the center of the pinwheel and stick it into a dowel rod or into the eraser on the top of a pencil. Blow directly into the center of the pinwheel to make it rotate.

After the indoor activities, have the girls sit down for the same discussion described earlier with the nature walk. Use a stick or perhaps a vine with some branches for a visual aid.

3. Time to eat!

Invite everyone to sit on a quilt for an indoor or outdoor picnic and serve them a fresh plate of flowers (see food section). Instead of using a quilt, you may want to cut inexpensive plastic table cloths into the shape of giant flowers for the girls to sit on.

4. Planting a garden

Give each girl her very own planter. Label the planters with each guest's name ahead of time so that they do not get mixed up. For the planting box I suggest a plastic planter's box or a bread pan made of foil. Make sure there are several small holes in the bottom of the pan and put a layer of small rocks in the bottom of the planter to facilitate drainage. Fill each planter halfway with potting soil.

Show the girls the picture of the flowers on the seed pouches, and let the girls try to guess if the seeds will be big or small. Let each girl have a work area. Use newspaper to cover the table or floor and to make cleanup easier. The girls can plant their own combinations of seeds. Be sure they understand the guidelines for planting each particular seed. After they have placed their seeds, let them fill the rest of their planter with potting soil.

Take the planters outside and place them in the yard. Give each girl a cup and tell her to water her seeds lightly. Encourage the girls not to water too much since they will be taking these plants home in a few minutes. Use the remaining time to open presents and hand out favors.

FOOD:

Flower sandwiches—Make your favorite sandwiches and cut them into circles to make the center of the flower. Use slices of grapes, carrots, oranges, or apples to make flower petals. A stalk of celery makes a perfect stem. Arrange pretzel sticks at the bottom of each plate for the ground.

Lemonade—Serve it with a real or paper flower sticking out of the top of a straw.

Ice cream—Soften a favorite flavor of ice cream and use it to fill up small, clean clay pots. Put a piece of wax paper in the bottom of each pot to prevent ice cream leaking from the hole in the bottom. Sprinkle crushed chocolate cookies on top to look like dirt. Refreeze. Put an artificial flower in the pot before serving. Make this treat one day ahead of time to give the ice cream time to freeze. If this is a birthday occasion, provide a cake with flowers on it as well.

FAVORS: Pick and choose from the following:

1. Favor bags—Use pastel colored gift bags with flower stickers on the side, or consider a basket or a canvas bag.
2. Gardens—The biggest favor that the girls will be taking home is the gardens that they have planted during the party.
3. Visors—The girls decorated these during the first activity.
4. Garden tools—Inexpensive tools are available at hardware stores and nurseries. Look around the store to see what is on sale. You may even find a good deal on some garden gloves which would make cute favors. Paint the girls' names on the tools or gloves.
5. Seeds—Give the girls some flower or vegetable seeds that they can take to plant in a garden at home.
6. Candy—Gummy worms of course!
7. Flower necklaces, pin wheels, balloons, and flowers
8. Hair bows or headbands made with ribbon and artificial flowers
9. Potpourri—Purchase a bag of potpourri. Put a handful into a small square of netting and tie up the bundle with a ribbon. The girls can use them as sachets to put in their clothes drawer at home.
10. Inexpensive floral perfume, bubble bath, or hand lotion—There are brands made especially for little girls.

* 12 *

International Party

Fly the friendly international skies to countries all over the world at this party. This is a wonderful opportunity to learn about and appreciate people from different lands. Your guests will wear something that represents a foreign country, and they will experience food, crafts and games from places all around the world. The theme verse will be Mark 16:15: "Go into all the world and preach the gospel to every creature."

> **Suggested Size:** 5 to 15 kids
> **Suggested Time of Day:** morning or afternoon
> **Type:** boys, girls, or both

YOU WILL NEED:

- Poster boards
- Colored construction paper
- Scissors
- Glue
- Balloons and streamers
- Globe
- Bed sheet
- Inflatable globe or ball
- Items for different countries
- Grocery bags

INVITATIONS:

Make invitations in the shape of the world. Using blue poster board, cut out 4-inch circles. Glue on green construction paper in the shapes of the continents. Across the front you may want to write *He's got the whole world in His hands!* The other side of the invitation should read:

> **Join us for some international fun on**
>   __(time and date)__
> _____ _____ **th birthday!**
>   (child's name)
> **Meet at:** _____
>   (address)
>   __(time and date)__
> **RSVP** _____
> **Please wear clothes that represent a foreign country.**

DECORATIONS:

Your decorations will vary according to the countries that you choose to represent. For general decorations, use about one or two dozen green and blue balloons to keep with the globe theme.

Around the party room, set up several stations representing different countries. Make a flag (or color one on poster board) for each of the countries you have chosen. The encyclopedia can help you to find the flag designs. Decorate each station with streamers that are the same colors as the country's flag and use other paraphernalia that you can collect from the countries. Use small, inexpensive cups and napkins for drinks at each station. Serve birthday cake on blue or green plates. Make name tags in the form of small globes or flags from different countries.

SCHEDULE: 2 hours

15 minutes—Arrive, make craft
15 minutes—Globe talk
60 minutes—Fly to countries
30 minutes—Cake and presents

ACTIVITIES:

1. Arrive, make craft

As the children arrive, hand them their name tags and help them to put them on. Point out the craft project and ask each guest to go over and join the others. Your main craft project will be creating a globe out of blue and green clay. Use the recipe below:

1 cup salt
$\frac{1}{2}$ cup cornstarch
$\frac{3}{4}$ cup cold water
food coloring

Stir all ingredients together over low heat. Stir constantly to prevent burning. In 2 or 3 minutes it will thicken and can no longer be stirred. Turn the mixture onto waxed paper or aluminum foil and let it cool. When cool, knead until smooth. After forming the figures, allow them to air-dry.

You will be able to make four globes out of this recipe. Make enough blue clay for every guest to have a globe. For green clay, make only one or two batches of clay for the entire group.

Let the kids play with the blue clay at first. They will enjoy rolling the blue clay into a ball. Then use green clay to make some of the land forms. Provide a globe for the kids to look at while they fashion their own. Allow them to work with the clay for 10 to 15 minutes. After they have finished, tell them to carve their initials in their globes and set them on a shelf to dry. If you have ten or more kids, you may want to let them work in small groups to make a globe as a group.

You will need a second activity for the kids to work on after making their globes because some of them will finish quicker than others. I suggest a large poster or a butcher paper banner with the outlined letters spelling the words *He's Got the Whole World in His Hands*. Draw outlines of flags from many different countries around the words. Provide markers and crayons for the kids to color in the letters and the flags. Allow the kids to draw the outline of their hands and color them.

2. Globe talk

Try to find an inflatable globe for this activity. They are usually available at educational toy stores or check in the catalog that is listed in back of this book. If you cannot locate one, use a beach ball or balloon.

Gather the children in the center of the room and ask them to stand in a circle. Punch the ball in the air and tell the group to try to keep it in the air by punching it. You can vary this game by changing the instructions to keep the ball in the air by kicking or only using your left hand. Or let everyone hold onto an edge of an old bed sheet and bounce the ball on top. Don't let the ball leave the circle.

After a few minutes of fun with the ball, ask everyone to sit down in a circle. Use the inflatable globe or a real globe for your discussion.

Ask the group if they enjoyed making their own globe with clay. Mention how incredible it is to think that God created our world.

"What a wonderful job He has done. He has created all the different countries, with all different kinds of people, each with their own special talents and characteristics.

"Let's look on the globe to see where some of the countries that you are representing today are located." (Provide extra costumes for guests who may have forgotten theirs.) Ask the children to stand up one by one and tell what country they are representing. If they don't know, help them out. Show the entire group the country on the globe.

Read Mark 16:15 to the group. Talk to the children about what the verse means:

Why do you think Jesus told his disciples to go to all of the world? Do you think he just wanted the few people in Judea to know the good news about Jesus? No, He wanted everyone everywhere to hear the good news that Jesus loves us and died for our sins. He loves the whole world. He loves people who seem very different from us. If God loves all those wonderful people, shouldn't we love them too?

Let's learn more about some of the people from different countries. We are going to take a journey to four special countries, and we will do some activities and eat foods from each of these countries. We will need to take a suitcase on our journey.

Give each child a bag with his name on it. These can be simple favor bags, or you may want to make suitcases from brown paper grocery bags. Cut the bag across the middle leaving a hump for the handle. Cut a hole in the handle so they can put their hands through it. Open the bags before giving them to the kids; otherwise, they might yank them open by the handles and rip them.

3. Fly to countries

Announce "It's time to board our international flight. First stop _____!" Fill in the blank with the name of the country represented at the first station. Put your arms out like an airplane and let everyone follow you to station number one. The kids fly together to each of the countries unless you have more than ten guests. If you do, break into groups by giving each child a colored ticket for her group. Each group will rotate to the different countries, and you will need to have an adult to help at each of the countries. Here are some suggestions for countries to be explored. You may want to use the countries that I have chosen or come up with some of your own.

Mexico—Hola! Let's meet our neighbors to the south! In Mexico the children play many fun games. One of the kids' favorite games is the piñata. Purchase a piñata at a party or craft store. You can also make your own by forming an animal figure out of crumpled up newspaper and tape. Cover the figure with strips of newspaper dipped in a paste of flour and water. Allow to dry for 48 hours and paint with bright colored tempera paints. Cut an opening in the belly of the figure and stuff with candy. Tape the opening after you have filled the animal.

You will need a blindfold and a large stick such as a broomstick. One at a time, blindfold each child and let him try to hit the piñata to break it open. In using the piñata, enforce two rules: 1) The rest of the children must stand behind the line so that no one gets hurt. (Make a line with masking tape several feet away from the piñata.) 2) Set a limit on the amount of candy each child may retrieve. When candy is knocked out of the animal, usually there is mayhem to get the candy. Tell the children that they must wait until all of the candy is knocked out and then each of them may get five pieces. Any leftover candy will be distributed evenly, but everyone is limited to only gathering five. Once they have found their five, they must move away to allow room for other children. If you establish these rules from the very start, everyone should have a much more enjoyable time.

You may also want to do a Mexican Hat Dance. Put a sombrero or two on the floor, play a tape of Mexican music, and let the children dance around the hat.

Another activity or favor you can make available at this station is tissue paper flowers. You can make these ahead of time to give to the kids or let them make their own. Use sheets of bright colored tissue paper and cut them into 3-inch by 5-inch rectangles. Take eight squares of different colors and gather them together in the center with green pipe cleaners. Leave some pipe cleaner to be the stem. Fluff and crinkle each individual layer of tissue paper. The result is a pretty Mexican flower.

Serve nachos, tortilla chips with melted cheese baked on the top. You can also look for taquitos at your grocery store. Taquitos are tortillas rolled up with meat in the center and fried. All you have to do is heat them up. Have a friend help heat them while you are working with the games.

China—Tell the kids that Chinese people not only speak a different language, but they use a different alphabet and letters too. Show them an example of Chinese writing. Use your library or a local Chinese restaurant for help.

Introduce the children to the Chinese dragon game. The children line up and hold hands. You will lead the children around the room in a snake-like pattern. As you lead them, walk faster and faster until you are running slowly. The challenge is for all of the children to hang on as they go. Take turns allowing different children to be the leader of the dragon.

Make dancing color sticks. These are made with a short stick with ribbon or crepe paper attached to the end. Use a dowel rod or yard-stick for the stick and attach the streamer with tape. As the children wave them through the air, they make pretty designs that almost seem to dance.

Purchase chopsticks to hand out to the children. Check with some of the local chinese restaurants or a party store. Chopsticks are very inexpensive, and they make a fun favor. Teach the kids how to use them. Hold one in your hand like a pencil. This one will remain stable. Put the second stick under your third finger. This is the stick that you will move up and down to grab the food. The kids will have fun trying even if they can't get it right.

Decorations for this area can include red crepe paper streamers and homemade fans. Make fans as a craft if you like. You can even use some posters with some Chinese letters for decoration.

Serve rice or eggrolls. Make the rice ahead of time and reheat in a crock pot for this activity. Or buy the little frozen eggrolls that you can purchase at your grocer. Fortune cookies make another fun treat. You may be able to find some with Scripture verses. Since tea originated in China, serve some warm tea in small cups. Don't be surprised if the kids don't like the tea, it is fun for them to taste, but they do not have to drink it.

Africa—Explain that Africa is a continent with many countries and that you are going to learn about the entire continent. Talk to the children about all of the wonderful wild animals that are found in Africa. Ask them to name some of the animals that they think are in Africa. Lions, gorillas, giraffes, elephants, rhinoceros, and zebras are some they may mention.

Purchase some small plastic safari animals and put them in a bag. Let the kids, one by one, reach into the bag without looking. Have the player describe the animal that they feel, and ask everyone else to guess the animal. After it is guessed correctly, the player can keep the animal as a favor.

One talent that some African tribes are known for is making bead jewelry. Provide several bowls of colored beads and some string and allow the kids to make their own necklaces. Boys as well as girls will enjoy this activity. Encourage them to make creative patterns and designs.

You may also want the kids to experience some African music. Make drums out of coffee cans and oatmeal cans. Decorate the sides of the cans using construction paper and markers. Start saving cans early. Lead the kids as they play their own drums. You play a beat and let the kids copy it. If there are not enough drums, give some kids spoons and cooking pan lids or have them clap the beat with their hands. Let them take turns with the various instruments.

Use a safari theme for your decorations in this section. If you have any stuffed jungle animals or pictures of animals, set them out as decorations too. You may even use a safari scarf to hang on the wall or plastic safari hats. Since we are representing many countries with many flags, color some posters with zebra stripes to hang in the area.

Serve fruit slices—bananas, mangoes, and papayas.

Italy—Mamma mia, what fun we will have in this country. Since Italy is famous for its ancient monuments, historic ruins, and beautiful churches, show the children several pictures of these relics. You can find pictures from books at the library or brochures from travel companies.

You may want to mention that Rome is where the center of the Catholic church is located and that the Pope lives there.

Italy is also famous for its Renaissance art. Show pictures by Michelangelo, Leonardo da Vinci, or Raphael. There is so much rich biblical art to show the children that you may want to show them a few pictures and let them tell you what story it represents from the Bible.

Since Italy is known for its pasta, why not try some noodle art? Purchase several different shapes of pasta noodles and put them in bowls. Provide everyone with a piece of construction paper and glue (pour a little in some cups and let the kids use Q-tips), then let them create their own design. Set the artwork aside to dry.

Opera is another aspect of the Italian culture. Sing a song together like "I'm A Little Teapot" or "Rain, Rain Go Away" in a normal voice and then sing it again using opera voices.

Decorations should be green, red, and white in keeping with the Italian flag. Since the flag is such a simple design, you may want to make a few from poster board to decorate this section along with some streamers.

FOOD: Pizza! I suggest cooking a frozen pizza and slicing it in squares instead of pie shaped slices. Have a friend heat it up before you get to the Italian activities. Serve small cups of grape juice to drink or give the kids grapes to eat. Tell them to be careful with the grape juice!

France—Bonjour! Welcome to the country of France. Let us go to Paris where we will see the Eiffel Tower, Arc de Triumphe, Notre Dame, and the Louvre museum. Again, locate some pictures of these famous places to show the children. Tell the children that France is famous for good food and art.

Give the children an opportunity to be artists. Provide each child with his own paintbrush, or if you can find some inexpensive water-color sets, give each child their own set as a favor. Roll up their sleeves or put smocks on the kids to keep them from ruining their clothes. Be sure to use washable paint. Let them paint a picture, telling them to do their very best work. As each child finishes, glue his picture to a larger piece of construction paper to make a frame. Set the pictures aside to dry. Be sure that the kids keep their paint brushes or paint sets in their suitcases so they can take them home. Wipe off their brushes before they put them away.

Your decorations can focus on the colors red, white, and blue since these are France's national colors.

Give each child a slice of French bread and a triangle of cheese. Serve punch in small cups.

Since you have four countries to visit, you will have about 15 minutes for each country. Feel free to rearrange the time or use fewer countries or fewer activities. I have packed you full of ideas so that you can choose which ones you want to use. Remember, at this age the kids are very active and need to be constantly busy. Some other locations you may want to visit are Holland, England, Hawaii, Alaska, or South America. Your library will be an excellent place to gather information on each of these cultures.

This would be an especially good opportunity to invite a missionary to tell about his or her country. You will want to have a station representing your missionary's country and let the missionary bring some items to show the kids.

Before you leave each country, have a short prayer for the people and missionaries in that country. Let the children volunteer to say prayers. Remind the children once again that God made each one of us and that He loves us all the same.

4. Cake and presents

Bake a two layer round cake and ice it with blue icing (white icing with food coloring) and green icing to represent continents. Make the top of the cake look like the world. Sing "He's Got the Whole World in

His Hands" as everyone stands around the cake. You can add the countries you visited to the song.

Next sing "Happy Birthday" to the birthday child. After everyone has enjoyed ice cream and cake, set the kids in a circle to open presents. Let each child hold the present that he brought. Call out the name of a country and let the child wearing clothes from that country come forward with his gift.

FAVORS:

The favors will be the goodies that the kids make and collect at each country. Don't forget to send each child home with a balloon and with her clay globe.

1. Mexico—candy and paper flowers
2. China—chopsticks and dancing sticks
3. Africa—necklaces, plastic animals, drums
4. Italy—pasta art
5. France—paint brushes, picture

* 13 *

Party Airlines

Party Airlines is full of high-flying fun. The kids will create and test-fly their own paper airplanes, then visit an airport or hear from a pilot. They will learn that God is the best pilot for their lives and that when they trust in Him, He will direct their paths (Proverbs 3:5–6).

All on board for a fantastic flight of fun! You can plan this party as a train or boat party as well.

➡ **Suggested Size:**   5 to 12 kids
Suggested Time of Day: morning or afternoon
Type: all boys or both boys and girls

YOU WILL NEED:

- Construction paper
- White paper
- Baskets and hoops
- Poster boards
- U.S. map
- Model airplanes
- Balloons
- Food
- Cotton

INVITATIONS:

Make invitations in the form of an airline ticket. Using blue construction paper, fold an 8-inch by 11-inch sheet in half lengthwise and cut about two inches off the top. Add some red stripes for decoration. On the front, write the words *Party Airlines*. Type the party information on white paper and put it inside the ticket cover. The information should read as follows:

One round trip ticket to

_____ Birthday Party!
(child's name)

Date of departure: _____

Take off time: _____

Gate number: _____

RSVP: _____

Send the tickets in a business size envelope. Write on the back of the envelope *Ticket Enclosed.*

DECORATIONS:

Cut four white poster boards into cloud shapes. Write the following verses on the poster boards (one verse per cloud):

- Psalm 139:8—If I ascend into heaven, You are there.
- Psalm 139:9–10—If I take the wings of the morning . . . Even there Your hand shall lead me.
- Isaiah 40:31—Those who wait on the LORD shall renew their strength; They shall mount up with wings like eagles.
- Isaiah 58:11—The LORD will guide you continually.

Glue cotton balls to the borders of the clouds to give a fluffy look. Hang two clouds from the ceiling or lights. Tape or tack the others to the walls of the room where the party will be held. Also purchase some inexpensive plastic or wooden airplanes to hang with string from the ceiling. Blue and white balloons spread around the room will add to the high-in-the-sky effect. Purchase paper goods in these colors too.

For a welcome sign, take blue poster board and write,

WELCOME TO BIRTHDAY AIRLINES
Flight #7 [or whatever the child's age]
Now Boarding

SCHEDULE: 2 hours

20 minutes—Arrive, paper airplanes
10 minutes—Paper airplane contests

60 minutes—Option one or option two
20 minutes—Airline meal
10 minutes—Open presents

ACTIVITIES:

1. Arrive, paper airplanes

Wear clothes that look like a flight attendant's uniform. Greet guests at the door by saying, "Welcome to Steve's birthday flight." Give each guest a flight pin. Before the party, call a local airline and ask them to send you some flight pins. If not, you can make your own using cardboard covered with foil.

Show the guests where to join the others to work on paper airplanes. Provide plenty of paper to allow the kids to create and experiment. They can fold their paper or try to cut their paper into the form of a plane, folding the wings and edges for reinforcement. Provide markers for decorating the planes. Check out several books from the library that show how to make paper airplanes. Lead the kids in a demonstration or let them glance at the books themselves.

2. Paper airplane contests

Hold contests to test the planes' ability to fly. Clear away furniture and objects in the room to provide enough room for landing. Here are some areas to test:

- Farthest flier—Let the children take turns throwing their airplanes. Mark the place where each airplane touches down.
- Longest aloft—Have all of the children launch their planes at once to determine which airplane stays in the air the longest.
- Aerobatics—Hold or hang a hoop from the ceiling. Let the guests take turns throwing their planes through the hoop from a distance of about five feet. Those who are able to throw their plane through the hoop will then try to throw their plane into a box. Create obstacle courses and tricks for the kids to try as well.

Don't forget to have a contest for most creative, most artistic, and most original planes. Everyone should receive a prize for some aspect of his plane. Prizes can be as simple as candy, gum, or award ribbons. You could award wooden airplanes or books about planes if you want to spend a little more money.

3. Option one

After paper airplane games, you have two activity options. If there is a small airport in the area, take the kids (with the help of some of the parents) to see the airplanes and the airport. Prearrange with the airport to have someone show the children some of the special parts of the airport and perhaps the cockpit of an airplane. Set aside some time to watch planes take off and land. Find a room or an area where the group can gather for a few moments of discussion.

Tell the boys that just as each plane is guided by a pilot who works the controls, our lives need to be guided by God. Our responsibility is to give the controls to Him. He knows what is best for us, and He knows how to guide us. Read Proverbs 3:5–6 to the group.

4. Option two

If there is not an airport that is convenient to the party, try to find a pilot or someone who knows a little about aviation to visit the party. Check with friends at your church to help locate a Christian pilot. Ask the pilot to wear his uniform and tell the children about flying.

Encourage your speaker to bring as many visual aids as possible. Suggest that he use Proverbs 3:5–6 as a theme when he talks to the kids.

If you cannot find a speaker, look for a short video about flying or just move on to the following suggested games.

The airport game—Pair the boys off with this simple game. Hold several long pieces of string in your hand—half as many strings as you have guests. Let both ends of the strings hang out of your hand. Each guest will grab the end of a string, and when you let go, each person will be holding a string with a partner. They will be partners for the Airport game.

One partner is the pilot, and the other is the traffic controller. One pair runs the course at a time. The rest of the players become the runway by forming two lines about eight feet apart and facing each other. Put obstacles in the runway such as books, boxes, shoes, chairs, and so forth. Do not use objects that will break or hurt the children if stepped on or bumped. The air traffic controller should stand at one end of the runway. Blindfold the pilot and have him stand at the opposite end. Now, the controller should verbally guide the pilot down the runway so that he avoids the obstacles and the people on the sidelines. You could also try this with two pilots and two controllers operating at the same time.

Air Traffic—To play this fun game, everyone stands in a circle, and when you give the signal, everyone must walk directly across the diameter of the circle and reform into a circle. The circle should look just the same as before only everyone is on the opposite side. After the children have practiced this once or twice, have them keep their hands at their sides and not bump into anyone as they walk. Strategies will begin to form. Some may walk fast as others take it slow. If a child does bump into someone else, she must say "beep!" Finally, everyone must try to walk across the circle with her eyes closed.

Fly across America—Pin up a large map of the United States and use two different colored airplanes cut from construction paper as markers. Place both airplane markers on Los Angeles and put five large stars on destinations across America all the way to New York City. Divide the children into two teams by counting off (one, two, one, two, and so on) and give them forty seconds to come up with team names.

Begin the game by asking a question drawn out of a box. If the team answers the question correctly, that team can move its plane to the next destination. The team to reach New York first wins.

The questions could be simple trivia questions about airplanes. Use some books from the library to help. Team members may discuss the answers as a group. Give only one minute for answering each question.

5. Airline meal

Sit down to some delicious first class food, served on trays as if on an airplane. Details in the food section.

6. Open presents

Tell the kids that the birthday child is the pilot and will sit in the pilot's chair while the passengers sit on the floor. This way everyone can see as the pilot opens his presents. Say, "Passenger _____," calling each child to bring his present to the pilot.

If you have extra time, here are some game suggestions:

Airplane relays—Kids will race against each other with one small stipulation: they must balance wooden or plastic airplanes on their heads, no hands allowed. If a plane falls off, the child must stop and put it back on his head before he proceeds.

Airplane dodge—Split guests into two teams and create a line with masking tape in-between the teams. Give each guest a piece of paper to fold into an airplane. Without crossing the line, the team members should fly their planes and attempt to tag someone on the other team below the neck. The tagged person must sit out. Remaining players are free to pick up any airplanes and throw them again.

FOOD:

Serve food on trays. (Begin saving TV dinner trays now or purchase foil or styrofoam trays from the grocery store.) Since you are using trays, you do not need to seat the children around a table. They can either sit on the floor, or sit on chairs set in a circle or in rows like an airplane.

Remember it is perfectly fine to serve simply cake and ice cream, but if you want to serve lunch, here are some suggestions.

Biscuit burgers—Buy small frozen burgers at your local grocer or make your own using biscuits and hamburger meat.

Carrot sticks or apple slices

Potato chips or french fries

Soft drinks or punch

Cake—Make your favorite cake in a rectangular shape. Ice with blue icing (white icing with blue food coloring). Use white icing or marshmallows to form clouds. Put small plastic airplanes on top of the cake. Airplanes can be found at toy stores or grocery stores. If you choose to serve cupcakes, put a small airplane on each cupcake. The airplanes can then be taken home as a favor.

FAVORS:

1. Favor bags—Depending on how much you want to spend, you could give small flight bags or make paper sack suitcases. Look around at discount stores to see if you can find a good deal on small zippered bags. If you choose to make your own, use a grocery sack and cut it across the middle, leaving a hump in the center. Cut a hole in the hump to form a handle. Make luggage tags with each of the guests' names on them and tie them around the suitcase handles.
2. Airline pins
3. Small plastic or wooden airplanes
4. Toy binoculars
5. Small bag of peanuts
6. Kites
7. Sunglasses
8. Frisbee or plastic parachute figures

9. Blue plastic cups or mugs—Paint the words *God is my pilot* on the sides.
10. Posters or large pictures of airplanes

Party variation:

If your child is interested in trains, see if there are any miniature train exhibits in your vicinity or go to a toy store that has a train display. Set out train sets at your home for the children to play with. Tell them that God is the conductor of our lives.

* 14 *

Ready for Battle

Is your boy a warrior? Why not put his fighting spirit to good use in the Lord's army? This party will be a battle of good versus evil. Each boy will make and wear his own armor of God. The boys will learn to use the armor that God gives them and play some fun games as well. The theme verses will come from Ephesians 6:11–17 which begins, "Put on the whole armor of God."

➡ **Suggested Size:**   5 to 12 kids
Suggested Time of Day: morning or afternoon
Type: all boys

YOU WILL NEED:

- Poster boards
- Foil
- Plastic one-gallon milk jugs
- Yardsticks
- Glitter, sequins, glue
- Brown grocery sacks

- Silver or gray spray paint
- Corrugated boxes
- Balloons and crepe paper streamers
- Food
- Favors

INVITATIONS:

Your invitations will be swords and shields. Use red poster board to cut out 4-inch shields. The sword is an optional item in the invitation.

Cut 3-inch swords from red poster boards and use foil to cover the blades. Or you could purchase sword drink stirrers.

On one side of the shield write the birthday information and decorate the other side.

YOU ARE BEING CALLED TO BATTLE FOR THE LORD'S ARMY!

Battleground: _____(address)

Battle begins: _____(time)   on _____(date)

RSVP to Secretary of Defense, _____(parent, phone number)

If this is a birthday invitation add something like "It's John's Sixth Birthday!" to the front of the shield.

DECORATIONS:

Shields and coats of arms will make up your decorations. Make these shapes out of colored poster board. They do not need to be detailed or elaborate. Write the verses from Ephesians on the shields. Use glitter and paint to add flair to the decorations.

Use red and silver balloons and streamers to decorate the rooms. Your cups and napkins should follow the same color scheme. You do not need name tags since the boys will write their names on their breastplates.

SCHEDULE: 2 hours

40 minutes—Arrive, make armor
20 minutes—Discussion and call to arms
30 minutes—Using the armor, combat
30 minutes—Eat and open presents

ACTIVITIES:

1. Arrive, make armor

Greet the warriors at the door by saying, "Welcome to the battle-field. Go prepare your armor for battle." Point out the work areas. If you have a small group, let the boys work on the same pieces of armor at the same time. If you have ten or more kids, you will need to break into groups. With groups, use several rooms for the work. You will need some other adults or teenagers to assist at the different stations. The boys will be making four pieces of armor: breastplate, helmet, belt, and shield. Let them start at any of the stations, but if you see that one station has too many boys, ask some of the boys to start at another location. Here are the four stations:

Helmet of salvation—You will use the plastic one-gallon milk jugs and foil for this activity. Start saving now so that you will have enough, or round them up from friends and neighbors. You will need one for each child. Before the party, cut the spout and the handle away so that the bottom of each jug forms a helmet. Have the boys cover their helmets with foil and make a cross for each side using colored tape.

Belt of truth—Cut long strips of poster board about three inches wide. Let the boys punch a hole at both ends of the belt and tie string through the holes to make a tie for the belt. Provide markers and let the kids write the word *Truth* on the belt and decorate it.

Breastplate of righteousness—Use brown paper grocery sacks for the breastplate. Cut out arm holes and a hole for the head. Also cut a slit down the back. Before the party, spray paint each of the sacks silver or gray. Set out paper plates holding sequins or glitter and other plates with glue and cotton swabs. The boys will decorate their breastplates with the sequins, stickers, and glitter. This activity would be best in the kitchen. Put newspaper under the work area to aid in cleanup.

Shield of faith—Give the boys a shield pattern made out of poster board to trace and cut their own shields out of poster board. Cut a rectangular extra piece of poster board for the handle. Provide markers and stickers for the boys to decorate their shields. You can use more glitter if you like. When they finish their decorating, let the boys attach the handle on the back with staples or strong tape.

Sword of the Spirit (optional)—Decide if you want to make swords for the battle. You know what the boys will do with the swords once they make them. It is not necessary to make the swords since the true Sword of the Spirit is the Word of God, and you will be talking about that sword during the party.

To make a pretend sword, cut sword shapes from corrugated boxes. Let the boys paint them with tempera paints (and set them aside to dry) or have them cover the blade of the sword with foil. Boys love the swords, and they may ask for them even if you don't plan to make them.

2. Discussion and call to arms

When the armor is complete, gather the boys together with their armor for a discussion. Start by telling them that the Bible talks about putting on the armor of God. Point to the verses written on the shields. Read to the boys from Ephesians 6:11–17. Ask them if they are aware that they have an enemy who wants to engage in battle. Explain that the Bible tells us that our enemy is Satan. Remind the boys not to be afraid because we are in the Lord's army and He has given us a powerful armor. Tell them that we need to wear this armor and use it. Explain each of the armor pieces and how the boys can practically use them in their lives:

The first piece of armor that the Roman soldier would put on was the belt around his waist. This belt was used to hold his other garments together and to attach the pieces of armor to him. It allowed him to have freedom to move his hands and legs. The belt of truth referred to in this passage reminds us to let truth be the basis of all we do and say. Honesty is important in holding the rest of the armor together.

The breastplate of righteousness covers a vital organ, the heart. We want to cover our hearts with right living. If we start doing bad things, eventually our hearts become dull to God. We must protect our hearts by doing what God wants us to do.

The Scripture tells us we must also have our feet covered with the gospel of peace. Even though we did not make this part of the armor today, it is still good to know about it. Roman soldiers wore shoes with spikes on the bottom of them during battle to help them stand firm. God wants us to stand firm with the good news of Jesus that brings peace into our lives and into the lives of those who receive it. We should not be wishy-washy when it comes to our belief in the good news of Jesus.

The shield of faith is for our protection. We can hold that shield up against the fiery darts that Satan may send our way. For instance, if Satan tries to tell you that God doesn't love you because of all the bad things you have done, just hold up the shield of faith, which reminds us that God loves us and forgives us because of our faith in Him.

The helmet of salvation covers another vital organ, the brain. Satan would love for us to think that there isn't really a God who loves us and sent His Son to die for our sins. He wants us to think that God won't really keep His promise to allow us into heaven one day. But when we protect our minds with the helmet of salvation, we are reminded that we are saved by Jesus and that God is faithful to keep His promises.

All of the armor so far has been to protect and defend the soldier. Then the Bible tells us about The sword of the Spirit, which is the Word of God. The Word of God refers to the spoken Word of God. We need this sword just as Jesus did when He was being tempted by Satan. Jesus always fought Satan by quoting Scripture (see Matthew 4:1–11). This is the tool that the Holy Spirit can use through us: so when Satan tries to tempt you, just tell him what the Bible says.

This passage implies that we are not supposed to go out looking for the enemy, but we are to be prepared for battle when the enemy comes. If the enemy does approach, remember to use your armor and your sword, which is the Word of God.

3. Combat

Lead the boys in acting out the battle of Jericho as described in Joshua 6 in the Bible. Remind the boys that it was God who fought the battle for the Israelites.

4. Battle games

The boys may want to take off their armor for the games because the armor can be cumbersome. Do not allow swords during the games.

Forcing the City Gates—Divide the boys into two teams by numbering off: one, two, one, two, etc. Have the teams stand in a line, facing each other. Team members should join arms to form a wall. Send one player from the other team to try to break through the wall. He is allowed three tries and can try to climb over, crawl under, or break through the hands. If he wins, he scores one point for his team. Then the second team forms a line and the first team sends a man to try to break through. Alternate teams until everyone has had a chance to try to break the wall.

Helmet relay—Line the boys up into two lines, one person behind the other. Give the first person on each team a helmet. When you give the signal, they will pass the helmet back through the team alternating over their heads and under their legs. The first team to pass its helmet to the end wins. Next, play with the boys by passing two or three helmets one right after the other.

Tail fight—Give each of the boys a piece of cloth to hang from his belt in the back. At a signal, each boy tries to snatch the cloth from the belts of the others. If a boy loses his tail, he must sit down on the sideline. You can have two winners for this game: the last boy to lose his tail and the boy who collects the most tails.

Human cannonballs—Have everyone form a circle, squat down and grasp his ankles with both hands. At the signal, the boys begin to push each other, trying to make the others lose their balance. They cannot use their hands. If a boy topples over he is eliminated from the game. The last cannonball still squatting is the winner. This game can be played several times.

Storming the castle—Divide boys into two teams by drawing numbers out of a basket. Have them stand in parallel lines, facing each other. Use masking tape to mark the lines where each team is standing. There should be at least ten feet between the two teams. At a signal, each boy starts toward the opposite line, with his arms folded, hopping on one foot. Each boy tries to get to the opposite line without being forced to put down his free foot or to unfold his arms. If he does put his foot down or unfold his arms, he is eliminated. Players can charge each other but not hold one another. Play continues until every boy reaches the other side or is eliminated. The team with the most boys over its goal is the winning team.

5. Eat and open presents

After the fun and games, it is time for some refreshment. See the food section for details.

If this is a birthday party, your son will open the gifts after the snack. Ask the boys to sit in a circle. Pile all of the presents in the center of the circle. As you call out a boy's name, that boy will retrieve his gift and give it to the birthday boy.

FOOD:

If you have chosen to feed the soldiers some lunch, here are menu suggestions. Serve on plates wrapped in foil to look like mess kits.

Non-sloppy joes—You will need hamburger meat, chopped onions, 1/4 cup ketchup, 2 tablespoons mustard, and one teaspoon of garlic powder. Cook the meat, drain the grease, and stir in the rest of the ingredients. Serve on hamburger buns.

Apples

Chips

Punch or lemonade

Shield cake—Make your favorite rectangle cake and cut it in the shape of a shield. Ice it with white or colored icing and decorate with candies to make a cross in the center.

FAVORS:

1. Armor—The majority of the favors will be the items of armor that the boys made.
2. New Testaments—Since the sword of the Spirit is the Word of God, you could give the boys a small New Testament Bible. A paperback Bible is very inexpensive. Or you might look for a small copy of the Gospel of John. In some Christian bookstores, you can find little two-inch books with key verses from the Bible in them.
3. Small plastic warrior or knight figures
4. Scripture memory cards for kids—Check with your local Christian bookstore.
5. Pocket cross or lapel pin—Pocket crosses can be purchased at Christian bookstores. They are crosses to be carried in the boys' pockets as a reminder that they are in the Lord's army.
6. Cookies or candy wrapped in foil

* 15 *

Time for Tea

Invite girls to dress up for afternoon tea. You will send out formal invitations to the young ladies asking them to join you for an afternoon of delightful fun. Activities include enjoyable lessons in etiquette, a lovely tea, and a simple craft. The girls will also take a look at a perfect lady in Proverbs 31.

➡ **Suggested Size:**   5 to 12
   Suggested Time of Day: 3:30 P.M.
   Type: all girls

YOU WILL NEED:

- Note card stationery
- Food, tea, and cocoa
- Craft materials
- Frames
- Favors
- Flowers

INVITATIONS:

Your invitations should be dainty, beautiful, and a little grown-up. Purchase formal note card stationery in pretty, pastel colors. If you are giving this party near a holiday, use the holiday colors. Write the party information by hand on the inside of the stationery. If you know calligraphy, you can put that talent into action. If not, ask a friend who knows how to write with calligraphy. Your information should read as follows:

You are cordially invited to an
Afternoon Tea
at the home of _____ (child's full name)
_____ (address)
_____ (day, date, and time)
RSVP _____
Please dress in Sunday attire.

DECORATIONS:

Most of your decorations will be at the tea tables. Pull out your nicest tablecloths and china and perhaps the silver service that you rarely use. Set your tables with tea cups, sandwich plates, and cloth napkins or pretty paper floral napkins. If you are worried about breaking or chipping your china, use your everyday dinnerware. However, when young girls dress up and are expected to act properly, they usually do.

I suggest a fresh floral arrangement for the centerpiece. Use the money you would normally spend on balloons and paper goods to buy flowers for the centerpiece and for favors. Many grocery stores have added a floral department, and you can find good prices on flowers and arrangements. Use carnations in vases to decorate other tables in the room as well. Give the carnations to the girls as favors when they leave. You may want to buy some daisies to pin on the girls as they arrive. Tie a bow on the stem for extra color.

Play classical music in the background when the girls arrive and when they are having tea. Pieces by Mozart, Schubert, Chopin or other classical composers are perfect to enjoy during tea.

SCHEDULE: 2 hours

15 minutes—Arrive, decorate name cards
15 minutes—Fun etiquette
40 minutes—Tea time
10 minutes—Reflect on Proverbs 31
30 minutes—Sewing craft
10 minutes—Presents

ACTIVITIES:

1. Arrive, decorate name cards

As your guests arrive, pin daisies on their dresses and invite them to sit down with the other girls as they decorate their name cards. The name cards will be used to mark their places at the tables for tea. Use 4½-inch by 6-inch rectangles cut from poster board or colored stationary post cards. Fold the cards in half to make them stand up. Let each girl write her name and decorate her own card. Provide markers, stickers, sequins, and glue.

When they have finished, collect the cards from the girls and randomly place the cards at the tables. It is better for you to arrange the seating to avoid any squabbles or hurt feelings. Tell the girls that you are not setting the name cards in any particular order and remind them that this is a wonderful opportunity to grow in new friendships and to mature as young ladies.

Another arrival activity you may want to consider is to let the girls make a felt quilt. Give each guest a 5-inch by 7-inch felt rectangle. Provide sequins, buttons, glitter, scrap material, and ribbons to decorate the squares. As the girls finish, staple the pieces together to form a quilt. Give the quilt to the birthday girl as a reminder of her party.

2. Fun etiquette

Ask the girls to join you in the living room and be seated. Teach the girls some simple manners that are usually required at a formal tea. There are some cute poems to help teach the girls.

Proper Posture

Sit up straight and tall.
Elbows to the wall.
One hand is a snap,
The other stays in your lap.

Explain to the girls that this poem helps them to remember that their posture should be straight and tall, their elbows should stay off the table and one hand is used for eating while their other hand remains in their lap. Mention that both of their hands should remain in their laps when not in use.

Table Conversation

Never a bad word about the food on the table.
Listen to others as much as you are able.

> Don't interrupt,
> Or be abrupt,
> And you'll earn a "Good Manners" label.

In this poem we are reminded of the importance of good conversation. Tell the girls that they should never mention that they do not like an item that is being served. If they are given the option, the proper response is "No, thank you," not, "Ooo, yuck." Tell them also to pay attention to what other people are saying at the table and never interrupt. On the rare occasion that they must say something, remind them to start with the phrase "Excuse me." Also, remind them never to talk with their mouths full.

Here is another conversation reminder. Ask the girls to try to say this verse three times fast!

> Please pass the potatoes,
> Please pass the peas,
> Please pass the pickles,
> For I need some more of these.

This fun tongue twister reminds the girls to say *please* at the dinner table.

Terrific Table Manners

> Put your napkin in your lap right from the start,
> Use your knife and fork as if it were an art.
> Be sure to chew your food with your mouth closed,
> "May I be excused?," the final question posed.

This poem reminds the girls to put their napkins in their laps and to carefully use their forks and knives. Demonstrate how to use the fork and knife correctly. If you are right handed, hold the knife in your right hand and the fork in your left. Once you have completed cutting the food, lay the knife on the edge of the plate and switch the fork to the right hand to pick up the food. Any food that cannot be picked up by the fork should be left on the plate. The final touch is the polite question, "May I be excused?"

It would be fun to ask two girls to volunteer for a simple demonstration. Tell one girl to be "Molly Manners" and let the other girl be "Susie Slob." Place a small coffee or TV table between them. Give them a plate, fork, knife, and napkin. Let them role-play some of the rules that you have just taught through the poems. Susie, of course, is the bad example, and Molly is the good example of proper manners. Let the skit go on for a few minutes.

After the skit, review the poems one last time by letting the girls repeat the poems with you. You may want to make a copy of the poems on nice stationery or colored paper to send home with the girls.

3. Tea time

Seat four to six girls at a table, if possible, but of course you will have to divide them according to the number of girls and the available tables. After the girls are seated, offer a short prayer to bless the tea and the girls as they grow to be godly young ladies. Your job will be to serve the tea and goodies.

4. Look at Proverbs 31

After tea, ask the girls to find a seat in the living room again. Open your Bible to Proverbs 31 or use a poster board with the important verses written on it. Decorate the poster with small pictures that help illustrate the verses. Focus on Proverbs 31:10–31. Before you read the passage, tell the girls that in the Bible there is a description of a marvelous woman. Ask them to listen as you read about her. For young girls (ages six or seven), I suggest reading a few choice verses instead of the whole passage. When you finish, tell the girls that we can look to Mrs. Proverbs 31 as an example of the type of lady that God wants us to be. Emphasize verse 30: "Charm is deceitful and beauty is passing, but a woman who fears the LORD, she shall be praised." Encourage the girls to work not only on their outward appearance but on the inner beauty that comes when we put our faith in the Lord.

At this time, give the girls a special picture frame that you have made for them. Before the party, purchase some inexpensive frames and decorate them with paint. You may want to paint flowers or bows on them. Inside the frame put a copy of Proverbs 31:30. Ask the girls to keep these frames as a reminder of the importance of being a beautiful lady both inside and out.

5. Simple craft

Here are several suggestions for crafts for the young ladies. Let your daughter help you decide which one to enjoy at the party.

During this activity, remind the girls of the verses in Proverbs 31 that mention the talent of sewing and working with the hands. If you have time, reread these verses (vv.13,19,22,24).

Stencil or stamp stationery—Buy plain colored stationery or paper by the pound and use stamps or stencils to make lovely stationery that the girls can take home with them. You can find stamps or stencils at art supply and craft stores.

Make jewelry—Use fake pearl beads and fancy jewels to make necklaces, clip earrings, bracelets, and rings. Purchase supplies at a craft store.

Decorate doilies—Purchase lace doilies at craft or fabric stores. Weave thin ribbon through the doilies.

Decorate collars—Sew a simple white collar for each girl and let her decorate it with ribbons, paints, and small jewels.

Decorate straw hats—Search craft stores and novelty shops for inexpensive straw hats. Purchase a variety of thick ribbons at fabric or craft stores to tie around the hat. Provide craft glue or a glue gun for the girls to attach baby's breath and other flowers to the ribbon around the hat.

Simple sewing—If you have older girls, teach them to embroider or cross-stitch. You could also give each girl some plain white gloves as a favor and teach them how to sew lace trim to the opening.

6. Presents and favors

If this is a birthday party, let the last ten minutes of the party be devoted to presents and favors. Before the party, remind your daughter to sit and open the presents like a lady and to say thank you after opening each gift. Ask the young ladies to sit on the couch or on chairs as they watch the birthday girl open her presents. If you have chosen to give flowers to each girl as a favor, hand them to the guests after the presents are opened. As you hand each girl her flower, say, "Thank you for being our guest."

Rhythm games are also fun to play if time allows. "Categories" is an old favorite. Girls begin a beat—pat the thighs twice, clap twice, snap twice. The first girl starts by saying a category and a letter from the alphabet. The next girl must say a word that falls into that category and starts with that letter.

FOOD:

Since this is an afternoon tea, serve light finger foods. You may want to offer both warm tea and cocoa, because young girls at this age have usually not acquired a taste for tea. Below is a suggested menu.

Finger sandwiches—Use wheat bread and white bread to make cheese sandwiches and peanut butter and jelly sandwiches. Cut off the crusts of the sandwiches and cut the sandwiches into smaller squares or triangles.

Scones, cream and jelly—Tell the girls that scones are a typical English delight enjoyed with English tea. Serve strawberry jam and whipped cream on the side. Split the scones in half, spread with jam, and top with whipped cream.

Scones

Preheat oven to 450°

2 cups self-rising flour
1 Tbsp. baking powder
Pinch of salt
2 Tbsp. cold butter, cut in small pieces
1 cup milk

Sift dry ingredients in a bowl. Rub in butter with your fingers until the mixture is crumbly. Make a well in the center of the mixture; add milk and mix with a fork to make a dough that barely holds together. Knead lightly on a floured surface until smooth. Roll out with a floured rolling pin or pat dough with your hands until about 3/4-inch thick. Cut in circles with a 2-inch fluted or plain cookie cutter. Arrange 1 to 1½ inches apart on lightly greased baking sheet; brush tops lightly with milk. Bake 8-10 minutes or until well-risen and golden. Cool on a wire rack for 5 minutes. Makes about 12.

Fruit—Sliced peaches or strawberries

Cake—Serve your daughter's favorite cake and decorate with icing flowers or real ones. Petit fours are lovely desserts too.

Tea—Serve flavored tea that may appeal to young girls such as raspberry tea, cinnamon apple tea, or orange spice tea.

Cocoa or lemonade—Serve alternate drinks for those who do not want tea.

Note: Let the tea and cocoa cool to lukewarm before serving. Young girls are still not accustomed to hot drinks.

FAVORS: Pick and choose

1. Favor bags can be pastel colored gift sacks with lace paper doilies attached to the sides. Write the girls' names in the center of the doilies.
2. Picture frames with Proverbs 31:30 written inside.
3. Craft projects
4. Carnations
5. Small bags of tea
6. Shortbread cookies
7. Lace handkerchiefs
8. Hair combs or barrettes—Decorate these favors with small artificial flowers.

More Expensive Items

1. White gloves with lace—Purchase inexpensive white gloves at a department store and sew lace around the wrists.
2. Tea cups—Locate some inexpensive tea cups at a sale or an outlet store.
3. Small baskets decorated with lace—Let the girls use these instead of the favor bags to hold their goodies.

* 16 *

Fantastic Football

Ready, set, hike! Let's play football! Boys will learn some of the "ins and outs" of the game and hear a testimony from a special guest. After a hearty game of football, the boys will chow down on a football feast. This is a super easy party to plan and put together. The theme will come from Philippians 3:14: "I press toward the goal for the prize of the upward call of God in Christ Jesus."

Note: This party can easily be switched to basketball or any sport that interests your child.

➡️ **Suggested Size:** 8 to 25 kids
Suggested Time of Day: afternoon
Type: all boys, (although you may have some girls who would love an all-girl sports party).

YOU WILL NEED:

- Several footballs
- Poster boards and markers
- Food

- Favors
- Colored cloth strips
- Balloons
- Chalk or flour

Note: You will want to locate a dependable Christian athlete to be the special guest at your party. First check with the athletes at your church. You may also try calling your local high school and talking to the coach who is in charge of the Fellowship of Christian Athletes or Athletes in Action. If there is no such organization, then contact a football coach at the high school. He should be able to tell you the name of a Christian athlete.

The guest will be in charge of two activities. He will lead the opening warm-up drill, and he will give his testimony after the game. I suggest that you repay the athlete for his time by giving him a gift or a gift certificate. And remember, most college athletes are unable to accept gifts. When you contact the athlete to ask him to help, make sure he understands exactly what you expect him to do and that you are depending on him. If he cannot participate, ask him if he knows of someone else who may want to help. If he accepts, make sure that he knows the exact date, time, and location. Send him one of the party invitations and call him a couple of days before the party. Suggest that he will need to find a replacement if he discovers at the last minute that he cannot make it to the party.

INVITATIONS:

Make football-shaped invitations. Cut the football shapes from poster board. Brown poster board would be perfect, but it is hard to find. Look for it at craft stores or art supply stores. If you cannot find brown poster board, then use white and color it brown. Use black markers to draw laces on one side of the football. On the other side you will glue white paper with the birthday information. If there are a lot of invitations, you may want to type the information and have it photocopied. Your invitation should read as follows:

```
                        Ready! Set! Hike!
Let's play football on _____(child's name)'s_____ th birthday!
Game day: _____
Kickoff time: _____
Stadium location: _____
Be sure to tell coach _____(your name)_____ if you can come.
   (your number)
```

DECORATIONS:

Whether at home or at the park, the decorations are minimal. Choose or have your child choose two colors—one to represent each team. Buy balloons and paper goods in these colors. Purchase two poster boards in the same colors and use them as team signs.

SCHEDULE: 2 hours

15 minutes—Arrive, warm up
10 minutes—Team names
60 minutes—Football game
20 minutes—Snacks and testimony
15 minutes—Cake, presents, and favors

ACTIVITIES:

1. Arrive, warm up

Greet your guests as they arrive. Let them reach into a bag and pull out a piece of cloth. In the bag you should have an equal number of two-foot cloth strips in the chosen colors. The color that the boy chooses as he reaches into the bag will randomly determine which team is his. Once the color strip has been chosen, cut the strip in half. The boys should stick the strips in their pockets. Let the boys toss around the football a while as they wait for more of the kids to arrive.

Start the warm-up drills once you see that most everyone is present. Ask your special guest to lead the boys in some of the drills that he does at his own football practice.

2. Team names

Give each group two minutes to decide on a team name. Once they have come up with a name, write it on their poster board.

3. Football game

Now it is time for some flag football. Mark 20-yard intervals with flour or marking chalk. Try to locate some cones to indicate the goal lines.

Generally you will want to have between seven and nine players on a team. If you have more than nine on a team, try to make two simultaneous games or have boys rotate in on different plays.

Assign an adult to be the referee and another person to be the time keeper.

Play two periods of twenty minutes each. Stop the clock only on scores or when time out is called by the referee.

Any member of either team is an eligible pass receiver. A player is considered tackled when one of his flags has been removed. The ball is considered dead at that point.

To block, players must keep their own arms crossed on their chests. There will be no tackling or unnecessary roughness. Impose a fifteen-yard penalty for rough play or tackling.

Most importantly, encourage the boys to go out there and have fun and don't take the game too seriously.

4. Snacks and testimony

After the game (or games), gather the boys together for some refreshments. As the boys are finishing their food, ask them to gather around so that you can reintroduce your special guest. Ask your speaker to take a few minutes to talk to the boys about his relationship with the Lord. Tell him to mention that competition can be a good thing if we play with the right spirit and give the glory to God. Be sure to give your speaker a time frame, so that he will know how long to talk. I suggest asking him to speak for five to ten minutes.

5. Cake, presents, and favors

A football cake will be the perfect ending to the party. If this is a birthday party, add some extra time to open presents. You can make it fun to open presents by pretending that you are the announcer at a football game. Introduce each boy with a title or position—for example, "And now here comes left guard Danny the Dynamo." As you introduce each boy, he can pick up the gift that he brought for the birthday boy and hand it off to him.

FOOD:

Hot dogs or hamburgers—If you are at home or at a park that has a grill, hot dogs or hamburgers would be super. If a grill is not available, bring meats and cheese for deli sandwiches.

Potato chips

Fruit or fruit salad

Lemonade

Football cake—Make your favorite 13-inch by 9-inch sheet cake. Cut away the corners to form a football shape. Frost the top and sides with chocolate icing. Use white decorative icing for the laces.

FAVORS: Pick and choose

1. Small plastic footballs—You can purchase these at most toy stores or athletic supply stores. If you are buying a large quantity, ask for a discount.
2. Football trading cards
3. College or pro football paraphernalia—If there is a local football team that your community supports, then some sort of souvenir would make a special favor. Look for caps, buttons, pencils, pennants, cups, etc. Check with college bookstores and booster clubs.
4. Football key chains
5. Football-shaped erasers
6. Foil-wrapped chocolate footballs
7. T-shirts in the team colors
8. Wrist sweat bands

* 17 *

Make It, Take It!

Your guests will create, make, and take original crafts and art work at this exciting event! The possibilities for creativity and fun are endless. In this chapter you will be given a large selection of craft ideas from which to choose for both boys and girls. Kids will have a tremendous time together and gain a true sense of accomplishment. The theme verse comes from Isaiah 64:8: God is the potter and we are the clay.

➡ **Suggested Size:**   5 to 15 kids
   Suggested Time of Day: morning or afternoon
   Type: boys, girls, or both.

YOU WILL NEED:

- Sacks or bags
- Craft materials
- Food
- Poster boards

- Clay
- Balloons and crepe paper streamers

INVITATIONS:

The shape of your invitations will be depend on the crafts that you decide to make at the party. For instance, if you plan to paint T-shirts, make an invitation on white poster board cut in the shape of a T-shirt. Decorate the front of the shirt and write the words *Make It, Take It*. Write the party information on the back.

If one of the crafts you are planning includes painting, you can make the invitations in the shape of a paint pallet and attach a small, inexpensive paintbrush to the invitation. If you are going to be working with clay, cut your invitation in the shape of a simple clay pot. If the guests will be building with hammer and nails, make the invitation look like a hammer. Get the idea? On the front of the invitation write *Make It, Take It.* On the back or the inside, write the following information:

Let's have some creative fun at

_____ (child's name)'s _____ (age) birthday party!

Date: _____

Time: _____

Studio Address: _____

RSVP: _____

DECORATIONS:

The decorations will have two main colors. Let your child choose the two colors or choose colors according to the present season. Use some finished crafts as decorations to hang around the room. For instance, if you are making bird feeders, hang a finished bird feeder on the wall or hang it from a light. Decorated T-shirts or hats can be hung on the wall as well. You can creatively display any item that the kids will be making.

Purchase balloons, streamers, plates, and napkins in your two chosen colors. Make a welcome sign on the front door in the shape of a paintbrush. Simply cut the shape out of poster board and write *Welcome* on the handle. Or write *Welcome* on a colored poster board and tape different art utensils to the sign, such as paintbrushes, crayons, glue bottles, paints, etc. If you feel that name tags are necessary, make them in the shape of a paint pallet and put the child's name on each one.

SCHEDULE: 2 hours

20 minutes—Arrive, make craft bags
60 minutes—Work on crafts
10 minutes—Clean up
30 minutes—Snacks, discussion, games

ACTIVITIES:

1. Arrive, make craft bags

As your guests arrive, greet them at the door and give them a name tag. Show them where they can get started working on their craft bags. The craft bag will hold all of their finished crafts so that they can carry them home with ease. You can make these bags as expensive or inexpensive as you want. You may want them to use ordinary brown paper grocery sacks or you could purchase large colored gift bags with handles.

Let the children decorate the bags using markers, paint pens, stencils, stamps, stickers, or crayons. Be sure they put their names on their bags. Provide a special area where you can line up all the bags so that the kids can easily see their names and store their crafts.

Here are some more arrival activities for the kids who finish their bags early.

Scribblings—Break into partners by picking crayons out of a sack. The kids will become partners with the other person who picked the same color crayon. Make sure you have two crayons of each color in the sack. Give each player a pencil and a large piece of plain white paper. The point of this activity is to take the most meaningless scribbles and make them into something recognizable. Each person is to draw a simple scribble on their paper and exchange it with a partner. The partner must make this new scribble part of a drawing of a recognizable object or scene. After everyone has finished, have the players try to pick out the original scribbles and vote for the most creative drawing.

Foil sculptures—Give each child a large piece of foil and tell her to make a sculpture with it. Encourage them to think about what they want to make before they begin crumpling the foil. Award prizes for most creative, most original, most artistic, etc.

Shapes from Shadows—Pick partners again or use the same partners from the scribblings game. Give each child a long piece of butcher paper. Attach the paper to the wall and let one partner stand in front of the paper. Dim the lights and hold a flashlight on that child as his partner draws the outline of the shadow formed on the paper. The child in front of the paper can stand in a funny or silly position if he wants. Use as many flash lights as you have available, so that several pairs can be working at once. Once all of the pictures are finished, let the kids try to guess who belongs to each shadow.

2. Work on crafts

You can arrange this activity in several different ways depending on how many guests are present and the types of crafts that you want them to make. If you have more than eight guests, split them up into two groups to work in separate areas. You can create the groups very quickly by holding a bundle of craft sticks in your hand. Before the party, put a red dot on half of the sticks. Hold the sticks so that the dots do not show, and let each child take a stick. The children with the red dot will form one group, and the children without a red dot will form another.

Decide on crafts before the party. In this chapter are many ideas, but you can find many more ideas simply walking through a craft store, art store, or hardware store. Decide also how many crafts you will provide for each guest. Your decision will depend on the amount of time the crafts will take to complete and the amount of money you want to spend. Very few crafts will occupy sixty minutes, so it's best to provide at least two crafts. You will be amazed how quickly some children zip through an art project that you may have thought would take forty-five minutes to complete. It is always a good idea to have an uncomplicated backup craft for those quick kids.

Explain to the kids at the beginning the steps they will need to follow to complete a craft. Do not give out the materials until you have finished your explanation. As the kids work on their projects, be generous with the compliments on specific details.

Here are some suggestions for fun crafts:

Decorated T-shirts—Purchase men's large T-shirts in packages of three or six. Wash the shirts before the party. Buy fabric paints from a fabric store or a craft store. Put a poster board or grocery sack inside the shirt so that the paint will not leak through to the other side. You can also provide sequins and jewels that can be applied to the shirt using the paint. Provide pictures that the children can trace onto the shirts. You could also provide football team decals to trace onto their shirts and paint. Or you could make this a sewing project by providing ribbon or lace, needle, and thread.

Clay—You can purchase modeling clay at some craft stores or make your own. Provide several different colors and suggest figures for the children to create. Here is a good clay recipe:

Modeling Clay

1 cup flour
1 Tbsp. salad oil
1 cup water
1/2 cup salt
2 tsp. cream of tartar
food coloring

Combine all ingredients in a large saucepan. Use a wooden spoon to stir over medium heat. Stir constantly to prevent sticking. The mixture will be soupy for several minutes and then suddenly it will stick together and can be stirred into a ball. When it thickens, remove from heat and continue stirring. Turn the hot ball out onto a floured surface, and begin kneading as it cools.

Building with craft sticks—Provide each child with a pile of craft sticks and glue and let him build whatever he wants. You can suggest building a house, an airplane, a church, a boat, etc. You could also provide paint for him to paint his finished product.

Decorating hats, caps or visors—This activity may be more suited to girls, but the boys may want to make a sports cap or visor. Provide sequins, jewels, and stickers to decorate the caps or visors. Decorating sunglasses is another alternative.

Flower arrangements—Let the girls make their own flowers and arrange them in homemade vases. The girls can make the flowers using green pipe cleaners for the stem. Attach another pipe cleaner on the stem to form leaves. For the blossom, the girls can cut out shapes from brightly colored paper and put the pipe cleaner through the center. The girls can also make tissue paper flowers by taking several 3-inch by 4-inch rectangles of colored tissue paper and gathering them in the middle with the pipe cleaner. Fluff the layers out to form a pretty flower.

Make vases from juice cans. Cover the sides of the cans with construction paper. Color the paper with markers or decorate with glitter and sequins. You can also make a pretty vase by gluing different shapes of noodles to the can and spray painting the finished product.

Bird feeders—There are many different ways to make bird feeders. Use any resources that you have around the house. Milk cartons make ideal feeders. Cut squares out of two sides of the carton and put a string through the top. Or you could choose a big project, letting the children build a birdhouse or feeder with wood, hammer, and nails. Be sure to have plenty of adult supervision. Kids can also make a cup feeder out of clay.

Junk art—Provide a big box full of junk materials commonly found around the house such as spools, pencils, string, cardboard, bottles, bottle caps, paper tubes, boxes, old game pieces, buttons, sticks, etc. Let the kids create a sculpture using the odds and ends that you have collected. Suggest that they make objects such as cars, buildings, flowers, trains, people, and so on. You may want to give prizes for creativity and originality.

Windsock—You will need poster board, tape, and crepe paper streamers. Cut the poster into thirds. Give each child a third and let her decorate it. Roll it into a cylinder. Tape it together and then attach streamers to hang from the bottom. Attach a piece of yarn at the top for hanging.

Paint—Paint what? That is for you to decide. Maybe a wooden step stool, a birdhouse, or a shelf. What about a clay flower pot, a ceramic cup, or plastic boxes?

Make accessories—Let the girls make jewelry with beads and home-made trinkets. Decorate a bandanna using glitter, glue, and jewels. Make hair bows, pins, or button covers.

Decorate large plastic cups—Let the kids paint their names and paint pictures of activities that they like to do.

Wooden airplanes—Let kids decorate or paint them.

Place mats—Make place mats for the dinner table. Use large pieces of construction paper and decorate with markers, stickers, or stamps. Cover the construction paper with clear contact paper.

Make a terrarium—Use a large jar, rocks, potting soil, and plants. After planting, the kids can decorate the lid.

Glass jar container—Decorate a glass jar with paint and cover the lid with fabric. The jar can be used to hold anything from cotton balls to peanuts.

Make "self" posters—Give each guest a poster board. Let the kids make their own special poster describing themselves with pictures. Let them cut the letters of their names out of construction paper and glue them to the poster boards. They can draw pictures showing the things they love to do and the people and things that surround their lives. You can also provide magazines for them to cut out pictures. Have them write on each poster *God has made me special.*

Christmas Crafts—If it is near Christmas, make a manger scene or advent calendar, or let the kids make gifts to give to their family members for Christmas.

Plastic picture frames—Decorate the frames with paint.

Ink stamp art—Provide plenty of colored paper, stamps, and ink pads. Let the kids create pictures or make stationery using the stamps. They can also make thumbprints and create scenes from the thumbprints. Be sure to have some wet paper towels on hand to wipe ink off the kids' hands.

3. Clean up

Now take a few minutes to clean up any mess. Make cleanup time a fun game. Here are two ideas:

Divide the room into two sections and group the children into two teams. Give each team a trash bag, wet rag, broom, and other equipment they may need to clean up. When you say go, the teams race to clean up their areas. The first team to finish is the winner, but the area must be spic and span. Each team inspects the other team's cleanup job.

Another idea is to do the human vacuum cleaner. The entire group lines up at one end of the room. Every third child is given a trash bag. Some children are given brooms and others wet rags. When you give the signal the kids work as quickly as possible from one end of the room to the other, eliminating any dirt in their path. Time the group to see how quickly they clean.

Be sure to carefully set aside all art work. Use a special table to display the projects. If there are messy hands, provide several large bowls with soapy water for the kids to wash off their hands with. Give them plenty of paper towels for drying.

4. Snacks, discussion, games

Time to eat! Let the kids chow down on snacks and dessert or just birthday cake. As the kids are eating, invite them to take a quick look at the finished products and then have a seat in the den. You may want to offer awards for the artwork. If so, give an individual award to each guest. Invent as many categories as you have guests. For instance, you can award most colorful, most creative, most unique, best use of clay, etc. The prizes can be simple craft items or homemade certificates or ribbons.

Begin a short discussion by reading Isaiah 64:8. Use a batch of modeling clay made before the party as a visual aid. Tell the kids that the Bible says God is the potter and we are the clay. Start working with the clay to shape a simple cup. Tell the kids that God, our loving Father, has created us and we are the work of His hands:

He is working on us to shape us into special people for Him. Just like I can take this clay and work with it to make it something wonderful, God works with us. He has a plan for our lives. Sometimes we may need to be smoothed around the edges, and sometimes He has to work with us over and over again to mold us into the person He wants us to be.

Just as your art projects are a reflection of you, so we are a reflection of our heavenly Father, and our lives should glorify Him. He is not finished with us yet. He is always helping us to become more like Him. Remember this clay, and remember that God is our potter and is at work in our lives to make us into something special for Him.

After you have finished your discussion, tell the kids to carefully put their projects into their craft bags so that the bags will be ready when they leave. If there is extra time, play the following fun games.

Human clay—Separate into partners again. Have one person become a blob of clay and the other become the sculptor. The sculptor works with the clay and forms the clay into any shape possible without hurting the clay. Legs can be turned, arms bent, heads tipped, and faces can even be made into funny expressions. After all of the sculptors are finished, let them exhibit their work. Switch jobs and let the sculptors be the clay.

Steal the paintbrush—This game is similar to steal the bacon. Make two parallel lines using masking tape. Divide into two teams and have them line up on the taped lines facing each other. The teams count off simultaneously so that the players' numbers on one team will match players' numbers on the other team. Place a paintbrush in the center between the two lines. When you call out a number, each player with that number tries to retrieve the paintbrush and get it back to her side.

If a player is tagged before getting across the line by the opposing player, there is no score. If she is able to bring the paintbrush back to her place, her team earns a point. Call out two numbers at a time to make it more challenging.

FOOD:

Snacks or birthday cake are best for this party. I would not recommend trying to provide an entire meal since your hands will be full with the art projects.

Popcorn in several different flavors
Pretzels
Cheese with crackers
Sausage
Grapes or apple slices—Squirt lemon juice on the apple slices to keep
    them from turning brown.
Soft drinks—Provide about two 2-liter bottles for every five guests.
Cookies—Serve your child's favorite kind.
Birthday cake—Bake a rectangular cake using your favorite recipe and
    cut it in the shape of a paint pallet. Ice the cake with white icing and
    use colored candies to look like blobs of paint. You may even want
    to put a paint brush on the top.

FAVORS:

The children will be going home with their craft bags full of the projects that they made. Most of the money you would spend on favors will be used for the crafts, although you may want to put some candy in their craft bags too. You could also give them some inexpensive paintbrushes or water color sets.

* 18 *

Bookmania

If your child loves to read or listen to books on tape, he will love this party. Guests are invited to come to the party dressed as the main character from one of their favorite books. Each child will have an opportunity to tell about their special book. They will be introduced to a great classic and experience fun activities to go along with the book. The theme will center on the fact that the Bible is the best book of all (2 Timothy 3:16).

➡ **Suggested Size:**　　　5 to 15 kids
　 Suggested Time of Day:　morning or afternoon
　 Type:　　　　　　　all girls, all boys, mixed

YOU WILL NEED:

- Construction paper
- White typing paper
- Poster boards
- Snacks
- Favors
- Supplies for craft
- Bible

INVITATIONS:

Make invitations in the shape of a small book. Cut a 9-inch by 5-inch rectangle from colored construction paper. Cut three slightly smaller rectangles from typing paper. Staple the pages to the construction paper and fold to form a book. You may want to add a ribbon as a book mark. On the cover write *The Story of [name] 's Birthday*

Party. Leave out the word *birthday* if it does not apply. Type the following information for the pages inside the book and have them photocopied.

[Page 1:]   Once upon a time _____ (date and time of party) _____

[Page 2:]   a nice girl [or boy] named _____
                 lived in a house at _____ (address) _____ .

[Page 3:]   She invited her friends to come over for a party.

[Page 4:]   Her friends were asked to come to the party dressed as the main character from their favorite book.

[Page 5:]   They had a super, incredible time discovering great books, playing games, and making crafts.

[Page 6:]   They all lived happily ever after.
                 RSVP: _____

Put stickers on the pages in the book and on the front cover to add color and pizzazz.

DECORATIONS:

Books will be your main decoration. Stand your child's books around the room on coffee tables and end tables. Set them out everywhere you can imagine. You may want to borrow some popular children's books from the library to set about the room.

Make book posters using colored poster board cut in the shape of an open book. Use white paper on top to look like pages. A large ribbon down the center will make a perfect bookmark. On one book poster you will want to write *Welcome.* Hang the poster on the front door. On another poster write the theme verse, 2 Timothy 3:16.

Choose one or two theme colors for balloons and paper goods. Attach the balloons to the books around the room. Name tags can look like small books that are slightly open with the guests' names written on the covers. Cut a rectangle from construction paper and put a small white triangle at the top to look like the pages of the book.

SCHEDULE: 2 hours or longer

15 minutes—Arrive, make bookmarks
20 minutes—Favorite books
40 minutes—Introduction to a book
20 minutes—Snacks
15 minutes—The best book of all
10 minutes—Gifts and favors

ACTIVITIES:

1. Arrive, make bookmarks

As guests arrive, welcome each one at the door and ask him to tell you his name. Give him a name tag with his character name and real name on it. Point the way to the area where the children will be working on their bookmarks.

To make bookmarks, cut strips of construction paper or colored poster board and let the kids decorate them with markers and stickers. When they finish, put clear contact paper on the bookmarks to make them sturdy and durable. Punch a hole at the top of each bookmark and pull yarn through the hole to make a tassel. You can use fabric or leather for the bookmarks as well. An alternative project would be to decorate book bags. These can be expensive, but they make great favors.

Some kids will finish their project early, so here are a few games to play as you wait for the others.

Long, silly sentence—You will need a roll of business machine paper that is used in cash registers or adding machines. Unroll the paper partway and tell the kids to line up on one side of the paper. Hand each player a pencil. The object of the game is to create a long, silly sentence story. Each player is to write three words at a time. One by one, players add their words, connecting them to the words of the last player. Players can read the last few words before adding theirs, but they do not need to worry about making sense. After the player has added his words, he can move down the line and add more words at another spot. When the last player adds her words to the sentence, choose one person to read the sentence out loud.

Never ending story—Tell everyone to stand in a circle. Toss a small object, like a bean bag or ball, to a person in the circle. That person must begin to tell a story, something made up on the spot. That player then tosses the ball to another player, who must continue the story. The story can go in any direction just as long as it somehow connects with the last player's contribution. Do not break the flow of the story no matter how fast the ball is exchanged. The player with the object must say at least a few words before passing it on to the next player.

2. Favorite books

After some fun with the games, tell the children to gather together in the den and sit in a circle. Ask the children three questions about the characters that they are representing. Each guest will have a turn to stand up and tell: 1) the name of the book, 2) the character's name and what he or she does in the book, and 3) the reason this is their favorite book. Encourage everyone to listen to the person who is talking. Most kids love to stand up and talk to the group, but be sensitive and do not make someone stand up if she does not want to.

3. Introduction to a book

Now it is your turn to introduce a book. You will give the children a short overview of a classic children's story and follow up with an activity. If you feel uncomfortable talking to the group, consider hiring a storyteller. Contact your local library or look for a storyteller's association in your area. Or you may know a friend whom you could invite to tell the story. Another idea is to hire a high school drama student to tell or act out part of the story.

Here are three suggestions of books to work with: choose one of these or select one of your own favorites. The goal is to introduce and build an appreciation for one of the great children's classics.

Little House on the Prairie by Laura Ingalls Wilder—Dress up as Ma, wearing a sunbonnet and apron. Make these simple items yourself or ask a friend who sews to help you. Say to the children, "Hello, my name is Caroline Ingalls, but you can call me Ma. My daughter, Laura, wrote books that tell all about our family and our lives on the midwest prairie. Those were such wonderful and simple times. We lived in a wood cabin that Pa built. We had very little furniture and very few things. I will never forget the Christmas that our neighbor, Mr. Edwards, risked his life to bring gifts from Santa Claus to Mary and Laura. They each received a tin cup, a stick of candy, a heart-shaped cake, and a shiny new penny. It was a grand Christmas.

"We had to watch out for the wolves and the Indians. God was good to protect us from both. I taught the girls their school lessons at home using a small chalkboard called a slate. Later they used slates at school. Would you like to learn on your very own slate? Let's make one."

Give each child an 8-inch by 10-inch piece of black poster board. Cut out brown construction paper for frames. Let them put their names on the frames with markers and decorate the frames with stickers. Or buy small black slates for each of the children to decorate. This option depends on how many guests you have and how much money you want to spend, but you may find some very inexpensive slates at a toy store or craft store. Give the children pieces of chalk and let them write on their slates. Give a short lesson in math or English if you like.

For an all girl party, you may want to consider a small sewing project since this was another special hobby with the Ingalls. Use sewing cards for the younger girls. An all boy party can make covered wagons as a project. Cut paper towel tubes for wheels and make the floor of the wagon out of craft sticks. Use pipe cleaners and cloth (old sheets are perfect) to form the top of the wagon. You may even be able to find some very inexpensive plastic horses to go in front.

For another activity, take the kids outside and let them run barefoot in the grass as Laura did. Have some simple relay races such as running races, sack races, and three-legged races.

Charlotte's Web by E.B. White—Dress up as the little girl, Fern, to introduce the book. Fix your hair in a little girl's style such as pigtails or a barrette to the side. Wear clothes that make you look like a little girl, such as a jumper or jeans. Don't forget bobby socks and tennis shoes. Ask the kids if they have ever had a very special friend. Then ask if they have ever had a friend that saved their life. Say, "It was once said, 'a friend in need is a friend indeed.' That is what our special story is all about.

"I am Fern, and I grew up on a farm. We had many animals that lived with us on the farm. Once when our pig had little piglets, my dad was about to kill the runt of the litter just because he was so small. I ran out and saved that sweet pig. I named him Wilbur. We have been friends ever since.

"Wilbur had another friend who saved his life. How big do you think that friend was? It was a tiny spider. But just because someone is small doesn't mean he can't do great things.

"The spider's name was Charlotte. When she heard that her friend Wilbur was going to be killed for bacon, she thought of a plan to save him. Do you know what she did? She wrote words in her web, special words to describe Wilbur.

"The first time, she wrote *Some Pig*. People came from miles around to see Wilbur and the web. As you can imagine, Wilbur grew more popular as each new word appeared in the web. His life was spared because of Charlotte's hard work in her web.

"What a special friend Charlotte was to Wilbur. After Charlotte died, Wilbur looked after her sack of eggs until they hatched and the new little spiders flew away. It is important for friends to help friends."

The activity you will do with the children is to make spiderwebs out of yarn. Give each child an 8-inch by 8-inch piece of wood about an inch thick. Hammer six or seven nails in a circle around the board. Give each child several yards of yarn or string. Show them how to tie a knot around one nail and then weave the string around the nails to make whatever design they desire. Encourage them to try to take some pieces of string and attach them to their webs to create words.

Another activity that may be fun for your guests is to make knick-knack boxes. Just as Templeton, the rat in *Charlotte's Web*, stored away his goodies, the kids can decorate plastic boxes to store away their treasures. Use paints, stickers, and ribbons to make interesting boxes.

Add some fun to the party by playing games that are usually played on the farm such as wheelbarrow races, sack races, and hot potato.

Another fun book possibility is Robert Louis Stevenson's *Treasure Island*. Dress as the young Jim Hawkins for the presentation of this book. A dress shirt with rolled up sleeves, casual pants, and a pirate's hat will make the perfect costume. Introduce yourself as Jim Hawkins and tell the children about the most incredible adventure of your life.

"As a young boy, I helped my family manage an old inn called the Admiral Benbow on the seacoast of England. Our lives changed forever after a strange seaman came and stayed at the inn. Eventually, I ended up hunting for pirate treasure on Treasure Island. My life was in danger often because of Long John Silver and his vicious mutiny. By God's grace several of us made it back with the treasure. Boy, am I glad that adventure is over! It was a great time, though, and I'll never forget the challenges we faced on Treasure Island."

Let your guests make pirates' eye patches out of black construction paper and thin black elastic. Use two pieces of construction paper glued together to make the patches sturdy. Now give each child a treasure map you have made of your house or backyard. The map should lead them to a stack of empty treasure boxes. Let them decorate the treasure boxes with glitter and sequins, stickers or construction paper. With older boys, you may want to let them build their own boxes out of thin wood, using a hammer and some small nails.

Next, the kids will need to find the treasure for their boxes. Hide a multitude of pennies all around the house or yard. Tell the kids to gather the pennies and put them in their boxes. You may want to set a limit on the number of pennies each one can collect. Once all the pennies have been found, take everyone to the kitchen to shine the treasure pennies. Let the kids drop the pennies in a solution of 4 tablespoons salt and ½ cup vinegar. Give each guest a cup of this solution and some paper towels for drying. The kids will enjoy taking home their own special treasure chests.

Other books or series to consider are:

- *The Chronicles of Narnia*
- *The Wind in the Willows*
- *The Secret Garden*
- *The Little Princess*
- *Anne of Green Gables*
- *Where the Red Fern Grows*
- *Nancy Drew Mysteries*
- *Hardy Boys*
- *The Adventures of Tom Sawyer*
- *Old Yeller*

4. Time to eat

You can just provide cake or add some snacks. In the food section I have suggested foods that follow the theme of the books. Your cake will be in the shape of an open book. See the food section for ideas.

5. The best book of all

After eating, tell the kids to gather around because you want to show them the greatest book ever written. Wrap your Bible in wrapping paper or put it in a gift sack. Tell the children that within this package is the most incredible book ever written.

This best-seller holds some of the most fantastic stories ever told. There is adventure, romance, warfare, suffering, and hope. It was written over a period of hundreds of years by many different people, yet it was inspired by one author. It holds the answers to life's most important questions.

Can anyone guess the title of this marvelous book? You are right! It is the Bible. There is no other book like it. How many of you have ever read the Bible or heard stories from it? If we have been given such a wonderful book, don't you think we ought to spend some time reading it?

I want to encourage each of you to read this wonderful book and listen to what it has to say. Second Timothy 3:16 says, "All Scripture is given by inspiration of God." How wonderful to think that we have God's message right here for us to read!"

6. Gifts and favors

If this is a birthday party, spend the last ten minutes opening gifts. Ask the children to sit in a circle. Open a book that you have covered with a fake construction paper cover. Title the book,   **(child's name)'s**

Birthday Party. Act as though you are reading. "Once upon a time, _____ had his _____th birthday party with all of his friends. They all had a fun time hearing about some super books, eating a book cake, and learning about the best book of all. Now the children have brought gifts for the birthday boy to open. John gave his gift first. [Let John take his gift to the birthday child.] Then came Sam. Next was Susie." Continue until each child has presented his gift. End the story by telling the children about the favor they will receive and say, "And they lived happily ever after."

Here are some more games that you can play if you have time at the end.

Acting adverbs—Choose one player to leave the room. Have the rest of the group select an adverb such as *slowly*, *nervously*, or *gladly*.

Once an adverb has been picked, ask the person to come back into the room. The person who left the room must try to guess the word by asking members of the group to perform an action to demonstrate the adverb. For example, the person may say, "Walk in the manner of the adverb," or "Shake hands in the manner of the adverb." The person can keep asking questions until they guess the word. If it seems to be too difficult for the person, the group can give more clues through their actions.

The minister's cat—This game has been around for years but is always fun, especially at parties. Have everyone sit in a circle. The object of the game is to think of adjectives to describe the minister's cat. Each new adjective must begin with a different letter of the alphabet, starting with the letter *A* and continuing through *Z*. It is fun and helpful for the players to tap a soft rhythm on their knees. Each person should be prepared with a new word when his or her turn comes so that the rhythm is not broken. The rhythm goes like this, with emphasis on the capitalized syllables: "The MIN-ister's CAT is a _____ CAT." Emphasize the adjective too. A variation of this game would be to use adjectives that all begin with the same letter.

FOOD:

As I suggested earlier, if you want to provide snacks, let the kids experience some of the types of food that may have been eaten by the characters in the book that you reviewed. Here are proposed menus for the three books I presented.

Little House on the Prairie menu—Serve corn bread, beef jerky, and beans. Kids seem to enjoy trying to eat beef jerky. Another food to consider is roast chicken. It is inexpensive and most kids like it. Provide lemonade to drink. Check your local library or bookstore for the *Little House on the Prairie Cookbook.*

Charlotte's Web menu—Prepare food from the farm, but don't serve ham or bacon! For snacks, serve apples, cheese, homemade bread, and hard boiled eggs. Mention to the children that these are all foods that might be served on a farm.

Treasure Island menu—Apples and foods with a fishing theme: gold-fish crackers, gummy worms, and fishsticks with potato chips.

Cake—Bake two small rectangular cakes and place them side by side. Ice the cakes with white icing. The rise in the center of each cake will look like the curve of pages in a book. Draw a thin line down the center with black icing and put squiggly black lines on the pages to look like words. Draw vertical lines on the sides to look like pages. You may want to attach a ribbon for a bookmark. Use another color as a rim at the bottom of the cake to look like the cover of the book.

FAVORS: Pick and choose

1. Crafts—One of the favors will be the crafts that the children make to go along with the book you present.
2. Paperback book—Give the children a copy of a classic to take home. Check with discount bookstores and try to get a quantity discount or go to a used bookstore. Many times I find wonderful books in used bookstores that look like new. Keep an eye out for bargains that you can find at discount stores. You do not need to give each child the same book.
3. Canvas book bags—These bags can be expensive, but if you do not have too many guests, they make special favors. You could also decorate and paint the bags during the party.
4. Small paperback Bibles or New Testaments—Since you are teaching that the Bible is the best book of all, you may want to send your guests home with one.
5. Bookmarks—Make bookmarks at the party or buy inexpensive ones.
6. Fancy note pads, pencils and erasers

* 19 *

Magic Music

Music is fun and inspiring! The kids will make their own instruments and use them to play their favorite songs. Fun music and rhythm games will be part of this harmonious event. Please note, you do not need to be musically talented to have this party. Our theme comes from Ephesians 5:19 where Paul encourages Christians to sing and make melody in their hearts to the Lord.

➡ **Suggested Size:** 5 to 15 kids
Suggested Time of Day: morning or afternoon
Type: All girls or all boys. My experience has been that children at this age feel intimidated with music and singing when they are around the opposite sex.

YOU WILL NEED:

- Black poster boards
- Coffee and oatmeal cans
- Shoe and cigar boxes
- Paper towel tubes or plastic milk jugs
- Paper plates
- Yarn
- Construction paper
- Markers
- Glitter and glue
- Hole puncher
- Boxes and box tops
- Rubber bands
- Balloons and crepe paper streamers
- Toilet paper rolls
- Food
- Favors

INVITATIONS:

Make invitations in the shape of musical notes. Use black poster board to cut 5-inch by 3-inch musical notes. Attach a square of white paper to fit on the note with the party information written as you see below.

LET'S MAKE SOME MAGICAL MUSIC

At _____ (child's name) _____ birthday party.

Concert date and time: _____

Music hall location: _____

Reservations: _____

If you can find some stationery with music or piano keys, you may want to use it instead of the poster board musical notes.

DECORATIONS:

For a welcome sign, take white poster board and draw a musical staff with notes on it. Beneath the score write, *Welcome To _____'s Birthday Party*.

The party colors are black and white. Purchase balloons, streamers, plates, and napkins in these colors. Hang the streamers from each doorway to look like piano keys. Look at a piano keyboard or a picture of one to remind yourself how the keys are arranged.

Use black poster boards to make large musical notes and hang them around the rooms of the party. Be sure to have music playing as the guests arrive. Name tags will be in the shape of—you guessed it— musical notes!

SCHEDULE: 2 hours

15 minutes—Arrive, decorate
40 minutes—Make instruments
20 minutes—Make music
20 minutes—Snack time
20 minutes—Create songs
5 minutes—Open presents

ACTIVITIES:

1. Arrive, decorate

As the guests arrive, give them name tags and send them to the kitchen where they will work on a craft. Have them decorate bags to hold all of the instruments that they will make later. Let them use glitter, stickers, and markers for their bags. The bags can be large colored gift bags, brown grocery sacks, or canvas bags. If you are a seamstress, you may even want to make fabric bags with handles or ties.

To children who finish early, give them basic silhouettes of musical instruments and some markers. Have them trace around the outlines to create people, animals, or scenes from these instruments.

2. Make musical instruments

If you have more than ten guests, you may want to separate into groups and rotate to the various instrument stations. You will need some extra adult help in that case. Be sure to let your helper know what to do at her instrument station.

Provide materials for the kids to make four different instruments. Use the following suggestions or think of your own. Plan for approximately ten minutes at each instrument station. As the kids move from one station to the next, encourage them to play their newly-made instruments.

Drum—Provide construction paper, crayons, and cans. Have each child mark off the length of the can on the construction paper and cut out enough paper to wrap around the can. Before they tape the paper around the can, let them decorate the paper. Encourage them to make geometric designs or draw their favorite scenes to cover the entire paper.

Stringed instrument—You will need pencils, scissors, shoe boxes (or shoe box tops or cigar boxes), and rubber bands of different thicknesses. Have the children use their fingers to mark off four marks with three fingers between each mark. With scissors they should cut small notches at each mark. Now let them place a thick rubber band around the box at the first notch. Place the next thickest rubber band around the next notch, and so forth. Pluck or strum the instrument like a guitar.

Horn—You will need paper towel tubes, construction paper, markers, and scissors. Show the children how to cut construction paper to fit around the paper towel tubes, let the kids decorate the construction paper with markers or glitter, and then tape the paper around the tube. Or you could use foil to cover the tube. Cut a semicircle from construction paper and bend into a cone to be taped to the end.

You may choose instead to make horns out of bottles. Collect any type of bottle from around the house. Plastic 2–liter bottles or dish washing soap bottles work well. You can decorate the bottles with stickers. Be sure to provide a large variety. Blow air across the top of the bottles. Various sized bottles will give you different sounds.

Tambourine—You will need paper plates, a hole puncher, beans, markers, and yarn. Put two plates together and punch holes all around the edge. Color the backs of both plates. Separate the plates and put a handful of beans on one of the plates. Put the other plate face down on top and weave the yarn through the holes to hold the plates together. The yarn weaving is fun and looks the best, but you can also staple or tape the plates together.

3. Make music

Now gather the new orchestra together for a concert. Tell the kids that an orchestra is a group of musicians playing together. Let the kids choose their favorite instrument and play as you direct them. Lead them in some familiar songs or play a tape of their favorite songs so that they can play along. Let everyone switch and play some of their other instruments. Ask the kids to think of a name for their orchestra like The (your city's name) Symphony Orchestra or The New York Philharmonic.

Mention that music is very powerful, that it can even change your moods. Play some examples of different kinds of music on a tape recorder. Play relaxing classical music, energizing pop music, jolting heavy metal, and hand-clapping country. Let them see the difference and identify the emotions they feel with each type of music.

Now ask them what kind of music they think God wants them to listen to and sing. Ask what kind of mood they are in when they sing praise songs. Maybe that's why the Bible tells us to sing with thankfulness to God (Col. 3:16).

Sing some of the kids' favorite praise songs. If you know someone who plays the guitar or piano, ask him to help you with this part of the party. If you are at a loss to lead the kids in singing, use a children's sing-along tape from a Christian bookstore. You may also consider inviting your music minister or a children's choir director to help lead the singing.

4. Snack time

See food section.

5. Create songs

Separate the kids into three groups by using this fun activity. Let everyone pick a piece of paper out of a basket. On the paper will be the name of one of three instruments. Use simple pictures if the kids cannot read yet. Have each child act like she is playing the instrument on her paper and try to find the others who are also playing that instrument.

Tell the kids that they will need to think of a name for their group. Encourage them to be creative and think of a name that glorifies God. They will also need to choose a topic for the song or rap that they are about to create. I suggest writing on a poster board the fruits of the spirit found in Galatians 5:22–23. Give the groups five to ten minutes to produce a song or rap about one of the spiritual fruits. Let the groups perform the song or rap for the rest of the group using their instruments for accompaniment. Record the songs on tape. If you have time, it would be fun to play back the tape so that the kids can hear themselves on tape.

6. Open presents

If this is a birthday party, play this musical game to open presents. Set the kids in a circle and let each child hold a present. Start the music and tell everyone to pass the present that they are holding to the right. When the music stops, the birthday child opens the present that she is holding in her hands. Continue until all of the presents are opened.

FOOD:

You can serve food on white paper plates that have rippled edges. Every few ripples, draw thick black lines to make it look like the keys of the piano.

Instrument sandwiches—Cut your favorite sandwiches into the shapes of different musical instruments and let the kids guess what they are. They do not need to be perfect works of art. Try cutting violin, harp, saxophone, and flute shapes. Cut circles for drums and don't forget triangles for the triangle percussion instrument. Let the kids guess what instruments they have on their plates.

Bugles snack chips—These are an old favorite that have been around for years. They are little corn snacks in the shape of bugles. You can find them at most grocery stores.

Fruit slices

Cake—Bake your favorite cake recipe in a rectangular pan. Ice it with white icing. Put round chocolate cookies on the top to look like musical notes. Use brown icing or shoe string licorice to make the stems of the notes. Use decorative icing in a tube to write the words *Sing for Joy to the Lord!* at the bottom of the cake.

Chocolate chip ice cream

FAVORS: Pick and choose

1. Musical instruments—The special favors from this party are the instruments that the children make.
2. Decorated bags to hold the instruments
3. Inexpensive plastic harmonicas—These are available in the favors section of most party stores.
4. Kazoos—Most kids love a kazoo and they are usually very inexpensive.
5. Balloons and candy
6. Small songbook
7. Christian songs on tape—Sometimes you can find tapes at a closeout sale at Christian bookstores. They make extra-special party favors.

* 20 *

The Glad Scientist

No "mad scientists" at this party! Our young scientists are "glad scientists" because they have discovered that our Creator is incredible. Each experiment that the kids perform will lead them to a new understanding about God. The theme comes from Romans 1:20: we recognize God through His creation. Rest assured, you do not need to be a science expert to have this party.

➡ **Suggested Size:**   5 to 15
Suggested Time of Day: morning or afternoon
Type: all boys or both boys and girls

YOU WILL NEED:

- Posters
- Jars
- Plastic cups
- Individual experiment items

- Food
- Balloons and streamers

INVITATIONS:

Your invitations will begin with a business-size envelope. On the back of the envelope draw the face of a glad scientist. Draw a simple round face with curly hair. Beside him, write *The glad scientist invites you to . . .*

Make invitations in the shape of a beaker or vial. Cut the shapes from white poster board. Color a small portion at the bottom green so that it looks like the beaker contains a green liquid. If this is a birth-day party, write at the top of the invitation _____ 's *Seventh Birthday Party!* If it is not a birthday, write *A Glad Scientist Party.* On the back of the vial or beaker, write the information as you see it below.

Experiment date: _____

Experiment begins: _____

Lab address: _____

RSVP: _____

DECORATIONS:

The theme colors for the party are green, black, and white. Purchase balloons, cups, and napkins in these colors. Make a sign for the front door with white poster board and big letters. Write _____ 's *Science Lab.* Use your child's name or your last name to fill in the blank. Make a giant vial out of poster board just as you made your invitation. Copy the words to Romans 1:20 on the poster and place it in the room where you will be having the discussion. You will have various stations for experiments set up around the house. Decorate the different tables with green or black streamers hanging down from the table tops.

Make the cups in which you serve the drinks look like beakers. Use clear plastic cups and paint measurements on the sides of the cups.

SCHEDULE: 2 hours

20 minutes—Arrive, lab coats, games
5 minutes—Glad talk
55 minutes—Experiments
30 minutes—Snacks
10 minutes—Open presents

ACTIVITIES:

1. Arrive, lab coats, games

As the guests arrive, present them with lab coats and tell them that they are going to be scientists at this party. The lab coats can come from many different sources. The easiest, most inexpensive option is

to purchase men's white T-shirts and cut them down the front. You
may also want to check at a thrift store that sells used clothing to see
if you can find some bargains on old white cotton shirts and blouses.
If you are a seamstress, you could sew simple white jackets using
white cotton material.

Keep in mind that the lab coats are not absolutely necessary, but
they are a fun way to set the scientific mood for the party. Let the kids
write their own names on their lab coats using a black marker. You
may also want to make glasses for each of your young scientists using
black poster board.

You will need an activity for the children to work on as they wait for
everyone to arrive. I suggest having several jars full of different items
such as beans, coins, cotton balls, or marbles. Give each scientist a
sheet of paper with a list of the different items and tell him to write his
name at the top. Let him try to estimate how many objects are in each
jar. After everyone has made his guesses, count them out together. If
you are counting beans, use a scoop and count how many beans fit in
one scoop, then count how many scoops are in the jar and multiply
the two numbers. This will also reinforce your guest's math skills.

Another arrival activity could be to play Create-a-Monster. Use
standard size paper and a marker for each player. Fold the paper into
thirds. Tell everyone to draw a crazy monster head on the top third of
the paper. After a few minutes, tell the kids to pass their paper to the
person next to them. Have them fold the first picture under and draw
a crazy monster body and arms on the middle part of the page. After
that portion is complete, pass the paper again and have everyone draw
crazy legs on the third portion. Unfold the pages and display the crazy
monster creations around the room.

2. Glad talk

Now gather the children together for a short discussion. Explain
that they are glad scientists instead of mad scientists because they are
going to see how wonderful God is through His creation. Ask, "Did
you know that the Bible says that we see God's greatness through
what He has made?"

Read Romans 1:20: "For since the creation of the world His invisi-
ble attributes are clearly seen, being understood by the things that are
made." Talk to the kids about the significance of this verse:

This means that we can clearly see God's incredible qualities by
observing what He has made. That's what science is all about—observing what God has made.

You have heard of the mad scientist, but I think some scientists are sad because they spend their lives trying to figure out how the world came about. We are glad because we know that God created the world. It is such an incredible creation that we know it didn't just happen. God had a perfect plan when He made this world, and we can see His hand in even the simplest ways. I'm thankful that we have a wonderful God who loves us. It makes me glad!

3. Experiments

Tell the kids that they will be doing several different experiments. If you have more than eight guests, you may want to split them into groups. Each group will go to a different experiment and then rotate after ten minutes. You will need some help. Each experiment requires adult supervision. Before the party, be sure to instruct your helpers as to how to handle each experiment.

You should have time for about five experiments. I have provided seven experiments for you to choose from. Select ones that will fit the interests of your age group. If you want more ideas, go to the library or ask the school science teacher.

Bubbling over—You will need vinegar, baking soda, baking dish, coke bottle or jar, and food coloring. Take one cup of vinegar, add blue food coloring to it, and stir. Put one tablespoon of baking soda in the jar and place the jar in the baking dish to catch the overflow. Ask the kids to guess what they think will happen if you pour the blue liquid into the jar. Now pour it in and let the bubbles flow out. Ask the kids if they know what produces the bubbles. Tell them that the vinegar and soda react to produce carbon dioxide gas. The gas builds up enough pressure to force the liquid out of the bottle. The gas and liquid mixed together produce the foam.

Tell the children that there is a verse in the Bible that reminds you of this experiment. Luke 6:38 says that if we give kindness to others, it will be given back to us, "Good measure, pressed down, shaken together, and running over." Draw the analogy that the blue liquid is the kindness and mercy we show to others, and as we pour it out on others, it overflows back to us.

You may want to show the kids that the same thing can happen when you take any type of soda pop and put a teaspoon of salt in it. Let each guest try her own small experiment. You will need to give each child a bowl and a small plastic cup to set in the bowl. Pour your favorite soda in the cups and then let the kids add salt.

Sink or float—You will need aluminum foil, paper clips, and a variety of objects to sink or float. This experiment should be done in a bathroom where there is a tub. Fill the bathtub with water. Present different objects to the kids and ask them if they believe the object will sink or float; then put the object in the water to see the result.

After you have tried about ten different objects, ask the children what makes an object sink or float. You may want to explain about the displacement of water. Flotation occurs when the object weighs less than the water it displaces. Objects that sink weigh more than the water they displace. For the younger ones, you can help them see that flotation is due to a combination of the object's weight, shape, and size.

Now hold up a paper clip and ask the children if they think it will float or sink. Drop it in the water and watch what happens. Next, make a boat out of foil (you may want to do this ahead of time to make sure the boat is seaworthy) and ask the kids if it will sink. Put it in the water and let them see that it floats. Put several paper clips in the boat and tell the kids that the paper clips represent our lives when the pressures of life get us down. Sometimes you may feel that you are sinking when your grades are bad or a friend is unkind to you. Put the paper clips in the boat and say, "Jesus is the boat. He wants us to give Him our troubles and He will carry us."

Let the kids make their own foil boats. Tell them that they can be as creative as they want as long as they make their boat to float. Put small objects in the boats and see how long they will stay afloat.

Sensational senses—You will need blindfolds for each child, brown paper lunch sacks, tape recorder, and objects to touch, taste, smell, and hear. Ask the kids if they can name the five senses—sight, hearing, touch, taste, and smell—that God has given us to observe the world around us. We use our sight all of the time to observe objects around us, but let's use some of the other senses to explore today.

After you have blindfolded the kids, bring out a tray of objects that have distinctive smells. Try an orange, vinegar, chocolate, a flower (or potpourri), or peppermint. Hold the item as the child sniffs it. Do not let the kids tell what the object is until everyone has had a chance to smell it. After everyone has smelled the object, let them all say what it was and go on to the next object. You may want to have several samples and a helper to make the observation go quicker. After they have smelled all of the objects, let them take their blindfolds off to look at them.

Put the blindfolds back on and tell the kids that this time they are going to use their sense of taste to discover. Provide tasty items such as sugar, saltines, and lemons.

Another fun experiment to do is to give the kids three different juices: apple, grape and cranberry. Tell them to hold their noses as they drink and then have them try to distinguish which drink is which. This experiment shows how the sense of smell makes a difference in the way things taste.

Let the children take their blindfolds off for this part. Have them put their hands into paper bags to determine what is in them. Here are some suggestions for objects to let them feel: flour, cloves, play dough, gummy bears or gummy worms, string, cotton balls, or sandpaper. Tell them to describe what they feel without saying what it is.

Record different sounds on a tape recorder before the party and let the kids guess what sounds they are hearing. Here are some suggested sounds to record: hammering, sawing, airplane flying overhead, a child crying or laughing, a car horn, birds, a car motor, an instrument, leaves rustling as the wind blows through the trees.

You can end this activity by telling the kids that the Bible says we all have different gifts and talents. God wants us to use these gifts to work together as a body just like the different senses all work together. The eye should never say that he wishes he were an ear. We should use the talents that God has given us for His glory.

Clearing the Water—You will need red food coloring, bleach, eyedropper, and jars. Keep careful watch over the bleach; you don't want to have any spills. Demonstrate for the kids by filling one jar half full of water. Add two drops of food coloring. Let the kids observe how the food coloring disperses throughout the water. You may even want to show them the difference between hot water and cold water and how quickly the coloring dissolves.

Stir to diffuse the rest of the food coloring. Using the eyedropper, add one drop of bleach. Continue adding drops until the color has disappeared and the water looks clear again. Ask the children if they know what kind of liquid you added to the colored water to make it clear again. Tell them that bleach contains oxygen which is easily released and combines with the chemicals in dyes to form a colorless compound.

Now say, "The Bible says that we have all done bad things now and then. The bad things in our lives are represented by this food coloring. The Bible also says that even though our sins are red like scarlet, Jesus makes them white as snow. God has given us a way to be clean, and that is through faith in Jesus. When we trust in Him, He washes our sins away and doesn't see them anymore."

Separate the kids into pairs and let them each try this experiment for themselves.

Magnifying Magic—Purchase several magnifying glasses at a drug store or grocery store. If you can find small plastic ones, you may want to give them as favors. Provide a box full of objects from nature such as pine needles, a leaf, a rock, grass, flowers, roots, or bark. Let the kids observe the different objects through the magnifying glass. Ask them to choose one item and draw a picture of what they see through the lens. Encourage them to draw only what they see in the lens and not the entire object. After all of the pictures are drawn, put them in a pile and hold them up one at a time. See if the other kids can guess what the pictures represent.

Remind the kids as they observe the intricate details of these items from nature that it took an incredible God to design and make such detailed and beautiful creations.

Chase the Pepper—You will need a pie pan, water, pepper, soap, and sugar. Fill a pie pan with water. Shake pepper on the water. Ask the kids what they think will happen if you put a piece of soap in the water. Take a piece of wet soap and dip it into the water. The pepper will run away from the soap. Ask the kids if they can figure out why this happens. The soap remains on the surface of the water and pushes everything else to the side. Next, shake some sugar into the clear area, and the pepper will run back. See if the kids can come up with any explanations. I like to draw this analogy: sometimes when difficult or unlovable people come into our lives, we want to run away, just like the pepper. But God can give us a love for all people. He puts that love in our hearts. The sugar represents God's love in us.

Air pressure—You will need water, a drinking glass, an index card, liquid soap, a pencil and a toothpick. Fill the drinking glass with water and place the index card over the mouth of the container. With your hand on the top, carefully invert the container over the sink. What happens? Ask the kids what they thought would happen. See if they can come up with an explanation. Tell them that the air pressure below the cup presses against the index card to make it form a suction against the glass.

What happens if the glass is tilted or is only filled partially with water? Poke a small hole in the index card with a toothpick. Try a short pencil also. See how large you can make the hole before the index card falls. Put liquid soap on the rim of the glass to see if it will make the index card fall. What happens if the glass is filled with soapy water?

Remind the kids that just because we cannot see air pressure, it is very real and present. Since we cannot actually see God, we may sometimes think He is not there. Tell the children that God is always there: He is always at work in our lives. His unseen power is very real.

4. Snacks

Time to eat! If you want to feed the children more than cake and ice cream, let the kids create their own monster sandwiches. See the food section for details.

5. Open presents

If this is a birthday party, ask the children to hold the presents that they brought and sit in a circle around a coffee table. Cover the table with a white cloth so that it looks like a lab table. Call out the name of each child to present his gift, saying, "Dr. _____." Let the birthday child open the gifts on the coffee table as if he were performing an experiment or operation on the lab table. This way everyone will be able to see the gifts.

If it is a nice day, let the kids go outside and play freeze tag. The person who is "It" tries to tag the others. If a person is tagged, he must stand frozen until someone else touches him to unfreeze him. The person who is "It" wins if he freezes everyone.

FOOD:

Create-a-monster sandwiches—Give each child a plate. Provide all different sorts of sandwich food cut in geometric shapes. Use sliced cheese, bologna, bread, ham, etc. Also provide raisins, stick pretzels, carrots, chips, fruit slices, and shredded lettuce. Let the kids create their own monster faces using the food. After you have let everyone look at one another's creations, let the kids chow down. You may want to take a Polaroid picture of each scientist with his monster creation to send home as one of the favors.

Clear soda pop with green food coloring—The green soft drink is fun because it is fizzy and foams a little at the top. Serve the drinks in the glasses that you have painted to look like beakers.

Green globby cupcakes—Use white cake mix and add green food coloring to make the cupcakes. After the cupcakes have cooled, take them out of their cups and turn them upside down. Use the icing recipe below. Glob the icing on the top of the cupcakes and let it dry.

Icing

3 cups powdered sugar
3 tablespoons warm water
Food coloring

Take three cups of powdered sugar and slowly add warm water, one tablespoon at a time. Stir slowly until the icing is a thick liquid, not too runny. Add food coloring to make the icing the desired color. Using a ladle or large spoon, spoon the icing over the cupcakes. Allow to air dry for about an hour. Add sprinkles on the top if you like.

FAVORS: Pick and choose

1. Favor bags can be brown or white paper lunch sacks with the children's names written on them saying, "Dr. _____."
   You may even want to draw a beaker as you did for the invitation. Or use green gift bags for the favor bags. Draw the Glad Scientist on the front of the sack.
2. Magnifying glasses—Inexpensive magnifying lenses can be found at drug stores, school supply stores, or even party stores.
3. Lab coats
4. Magnets—Check with toy stores and hardware stores.
5. Fake glasses—Look for inexpensive googly-eyed glasses at a party store. The kids love them!
6. Balloons and beaker cups
7. Be on the lookout for other small favor items that have something to do with science. Little plastic telescopes or bug catcher nets are possibilities.

Ages Ten Through Fifteen

Recently, I mentioned to our junior high youth minister that I was writing a party book. The first thing he said to me was, "Don't use the word 'party' around the youth."

"Why not?" I asked in ignorance.

"Because they associate parties either with 'baby games' or with drinking and having a wild time."

He suggested several alternate words such as *event*, *gathering*, *experience*, or *happening*. Therefore, in this section I have used words besides *party*, just to be on the safe side.

Life begins to change as kids reach the preteen years. Their friends and peer groups become very important, yet they begin to feel less confident about themselves and their relationships. As you interact with and entertain this age group, be aware of their uncertain self-images and their need to feel "in" and accepted.

Notice that most parties are for mixed groups as well as all boys and all girls. These are transition years. Some kids will prefer mixed groups while others would feel more comfortable with all girls or all boys. Your son or daughter can help you decide which would be best for his or her group of friends. For parties at this age, it's important to seek out your kids' opinions and help in planning their parties. They can help with all the preparations as well.

This section is different from the first two in several ways. By the preteen years, the kids enjoy talking and mingling while they munch on snacks. It is not necessary to keep them busy every moment. Boys tend to be more task oriented than girls, so I have suggested games for them during the arrival time. Girls, on the other hand, love to chat and could be happy just talking through the majority of the party. Be flexible with the schedule to suit the interests of your guests. You will notice that with this age group, you can accommodate more guests. I suggest between five to twenty guests.

As guests arrive at the party, have your son or daughter greet them at the door. Encourage them to greet everyone with a smile and to make each guest feel welcome. You will want to have music playing as the kids arrive and during the party if it is appropriate. Check your Christian bookstore for some popular Christian music. Let your kids help you choose some music that they like.

Decorations are not as important at this age level and may be perceived as "corny." So keep the decorations limited and stay away from too many balloons and streamers. Favors are also unnecessary items. Generally, preteens have grown "too cool" for little gift items handed out at the end of a party. I have included only a few suggestions of favors if you decide you would like to give them. Preteens will probably consume more food and snacks at parties, so spend your money on these items rather than on favors.

The parties in this section are meant to be used for any occasion. Get-togethers, birthdays, or end-of-the-year bashes—your preteen guests will have a blast and will go home with not only a happy feeling but a spiritual truth as well!

* 21 *

Slip, Slop, and Slumber!

This is no ordinary slumber party. It is filled with fun and unique games, plus a lesson about slumber and laziness from Proverbs 6:6–11. The party will start off with coloring T-shirts that will later be used as nightshirts. Later, the kids will *slip* around as they do some foot painting, and *slop* their ice cream to create some fantastic frozen desserts. Lots of snacks and a little slumber will be included!

➡️ **Suggested Size:**   5 to 12 kids
Suggested Time of Day: late evening
Type: all boys or all girls

YOU WILL NEED:

- Butcher paper
- Paint
- Several dish tubs
- Towels
- Snacks
- Items for games

- T-shirts
- White paper
- Markers
- Craft items
- Breakfast food

INVITATIONS:

Make invitations in the form of a pillow. Use poster board to cut a pillow shape and write the following information on it:

You're invited to a
Slip, Slop, and Slumber Party
At _____ (name)'s _____ house.
Address: _____
Time and Date: _____
RSVP: _____
Morning Pick-up At: _____

SCHEDULE: overnight

20 minutes—Arrive, color T-shirts
40 minutes—Eat (optional)
25 minutes—Slip!
25 minutes—Slop!
60 minutes—Game time
20 minutes—Snacks and slumber talk
25 minutes—Partners games
Extra games
Slumber!
Breakfast

ACTIVITIES:

1. Arrive, color T-shirts

As the guests arrive, greet them at the door and give each guest a
men's T-shirt. Provide an assortment of colored, permanent markers
for the kids to use for coloring their T-shirts. Put a folded paper
grocery sack inside the T-shirt so that the marker doesn't go through.
The kids can draw their names or a picture or write *Slumber Party* and
the year. Encourage them to sign one another's shirts. This shirt will
make a great favor and souvenir of the party and will work as a night-
shirt for the slumber party as well.

2. Eat

Serve pizza or hamburgers—these foods seem to be two favorites of
this age group. You could combine the Pizza Party in chapter 29 with
this party.

If you choose to start the party after dinner, then this would be a
good time to make snack food sculptures. Provide four or five different
kinds of snack foods such as potato chips, corn chips, pretzels, popcorn, cheese puffs, etc. You will also need three 8-ounce packages of

cream cheese, eight ounces of sour cream, one package of dried onion soup mix, a mixing bowl, a spoon and plastic knives. Before the party, prepare the paste. The edible paste will be used to stick the sculptures together. Mix the cream cheese and sour cream and stir in a package of dried onion soup mix.

Divide the kids into groups or let them work as individuals. Each person should have a paper plate to hold his sculpture. Set out all of the snack foods and let the kids go to work creating structures using the food. Have contests for the tallest structure, the most creative, and the most original. After everyone has had a chance to create their own and observe the others, let them eat their creations.

3. Slip!

Now it's time for some slippery fun. You have heard of finger painting, well now the kids are going to try their hands—that is, their feet—at some toe painting. Ask everyone to join you in the garage or basement or kitchen—anywhere you can make a little mess—and tell them to take off their shoes and roll up their pants legs. Have a poster board or butcher paper lying on the floor for each child. Provide a chair for each artist to sit in as he works on his creation. Cover the floor under the posters with drop cloths like painters use. Drop cloths are available at most hardware stores.

Provide four or five different colors of finger paints and squirt a little paint onto each artist's paper. The object of this artistic game is for the kids to try to paint the best pictures they can using the untapped talent of their feet.

As they finish, have the kids dip their feet in a dish tub full of water. Provide lots of towels to wipe and dry their feet. As you help them clean their feet, you could remind them that Jesus washed His disciples' feet to show a servant's heart.

Be sure the kids get their shoes back on their feet before the next activity. Hang their artwork on the wall with thumbtacks or set them somewhere out of the way to dry.

4. Slop!

Now let's slop some ice cream around to make an incredible edible treat. You will need vanilla and chocolate ice cream and toppings. Provide a bowl and a large spoon for each guest. Soften the ice cream by leaving it out of the freezer for a few minutes before you serve the treat. Let the kids choose a topping to stir into their ice cream. Toppings can be items such as M&Ms, crumbled cookies or candy bars, nuts, sprinkles, or cookie dough. Let them make their own mixed up creation and then eat it!

5. Game time

Use the games I suggest below or play a board game or ball game. For the girls, you may want to refer to some of the games suggested in the Girl Time party in chapter 22.

Getting Together—In this game players will line up together according to the directions that you give. The players will need to get information about the others in order to put themselves in order. Here are some examples of the kinds of directions you might give:

- Line up according to shoe size, from biggest to smallest.
- Line up alphabetically using your last name.
- Line up in the order of hair length, longest to shortest.
- Line up by age, youngest to oldest.
- Line up according to birthdays, January to December.

Next, play the same kind of game by forming groups of people who share certain characteristics. Call out directions such as, "Find the others that have the same color of eyes." Other ideas for grouping are: color of socks, number of brothers and sisters, favorite ice cream flavor, favorite sport, and so on.

Human knot—Players join hands and form a circle. Two players stand away from the circle and close their eyes. The players in the circle twist themselves into a large knot by going over, under, around, and through the other players, without breaking hands. After a good knot has been formed, the two players outside of the circle open their eyes and try to figure out how to untangle the group. The group must cooperate with the two untanglers as they try to untwist the knot.

Twirling disc—The players sit in a circle on the floor and count off so that each person has a number. Put a Frisbee on the floor in the center of the circle. One player starts by getting up and spinning the Frisbee as you would spin a coin. As the player sits down, he calls out the number of another player who must jump up and get the disc before it stops and give it another spin. Then that player calls another number as he sits down. If the disc stops, then one player should get it going again. This game encourages cooperation in keeping the disc spinning, and it should not be a competitive game.

Balloon soccer—Move the furniture out of the way to create a playing field. Count off into two teams and let each team pick a goalie. Tell the kids that you will rotate goalies so that everyone who wants a chance will have it. Give each goalie a safety pin or tack. Have all of the other players sit down, evenly dispersed throughout the room. Drop an inflated balloon in the center of the room, and let the teams try to hit the balloon to their goalies. The goalie tries to pop the balloon. If the goalie pops a balloon, he earns a point for his team. Use twelve inflated balloons for this game.

Laser light—You will need a flashlight to be the laser and a chair to be the space station for this activity. Darken the room as much as possible. Choose one player to be the Space Patrol and stand guard over the space station in the middle of the room with his laser light. The person who is the guard covers his eyes and counts to fifty while everyone hides. The object of the game is to get to the space station in the center of the room without getting tagged with the beam from the laser. If a player gets caught by the laser, she is instantly frozen in space until the game ends. The first person to get to the space station without getting caught is the next Space Patrol.

6. Snacks and slumber

After the games, offer soft drinks and pretzels or trail mix. Ask everyone to find a place to sit down so that you can talk to the group. Begin by asking the kids if they knew that the Bible talks about slumber.

The same passage in the Bible that talks about slumber also talks about ants. Can anyone guess what slumber has to do with ants?

Proverbs tells us to look at the ants and learn from them. God is telling us to look to the ants because he wants us to see an example of hard work. God points out that the ants are not lazy or procrastinators.

Read Proverbs 6:6–11 to the kids. Ask: "Do you think it bothers God when we are lazy? What are some of the ways we are lazy? Are you lazy about homework or chores, or could it be in athletics, drill team, or practicing the piano?"

God tells us that if we are lazy and slumber all of the time we will be in poverty.

Let's learn from the ant not to slumber all the time but to be busy about the tasks that God has given us. Now keep in mind that God was not telling us never to slumber. We can still sleep later on at this party. He just doesn't want us to be lazy and slumber our days away; but nights are okay.

After you finish your talk, have the kids put their plates in the kitchen and get ready for the next event.

Partners games—Divide the group in half and tell one half to take off their right shoe and put it in the bag (use a pillowcase). Now have each person in the other group reach in the bag and draw out a shoe. The person who belongs to the shoe will become their partner for the next few games. If there is an odd number of kids, make one group a threesome.

Partner stand up—Have each pair sit on the floor, back to back, and lock their arms. When you say "go!" have them try to stand up without unlocking their arms. The first pair to stand is the winner.

Profiles—Give each person a pencil and paper. Instruct the kids to draw the profiles of their partners. Ask each person to write his partner's name on the back of the paper. When everyone has finished, gather the entire group together to try to guess which profile belongs to each person.

Tumble tussle—Partners sit back to back on the floor. Each one has his knees bent and his hands clasped under his knees. While in this position, his hands are tied with a handkerchief or a strip of material and his feet are tied the same way. Both kids seem quite helpless with their backs to each other. They each try to knock the other over. The winner is the one who succeeds. This is a fun game to watch as well as to participate in.

String games—Here is a girls' alternative to the tumble tussle. Give each pair a foot-and-a-half long piece of yarn with the ends tied together to form a loop. Let the girls try their hand at string games. Some of the girls may know some games that they can teach the others. Have the partners make up their own string games. You can also find books in the library with instructions on string games.

Interview—Tell each guest to ask her partner the following five questions. No pencil and paper are allowed. The kids must remember their partner's answers and tell the answers to the group.
    What is your favorite color?
    What is your favorite game to play?
    What is your favorite food?
    Where did you go on your favorite vacation?
    What is your favorite subject in school? You may want to write the questions on poster board so that they don't have to memorize the questions too.

Thumb wrestling—Each player closes one hand into a fist (both partners must use the same hand). Then they raise their thumb and open their fists slightly to interlock with the partner's hand. Partners should be clasping hands with their thumbs upright. The object is for one partner to put the other's thumb down.

Instead of wrestling, girls might enjoy painting each other's toenails and fingernails. Offer several nail polish colors from which to choose and be sure to do this activity in the kitchen or bathroom in case of spills.

7. Extra games

If the kids still have energy and no interest in sleeping, have some quiet games available. By this time some may want to go to sleep, including you. Quiet games can be puzzles, dominoes, board games, or perhaps building a house out of cards or a video.

8. Slumber

I suggest you have a cutoff point for everyone to get a little shut-eye. You can call it "lights out" at 1:30 and let them talk quietly, if they want, for another half hour.

9. Breakfast

Rise and shine about an hour before pick-up time. Send your spouse or another parent out to buy fresh donuts. Provide juice, milk, and some bacon. Some kids may want to go back to some of the games that they were playing the night before; others may want to talk. Girls will probably spend most of their time in the bathroom getting ready.

FOOD:

Slumber parties require quite a bit of food!

Dessert—Put toppings on ice cream and slop them together to make an original new flavor. Use vanilla and chocolate ice cream. The toppings can be nuts, chocolate chips, crushed cookies or candy bars, peanut butter, cookie dough, etc.

Snacks—Popcorn, trail mix, pretzels, fruit and veggies and dip, crackers and cheese, and don't forget the snacks for the snack sculpture.

Soft drinks—You may want to purchase four 2-liter bottles of soft drinks for every five guests. I know that sounds like a lot, but the kids may be drinking soft drinks all night. Many times they may fill up a cup, and leave it somewhere and then fill up another. It is better to have too much to drink than too little. Make sure you have plenty of cups too. You may want to label the cups so that the kids can keep up with their own. Later in the evening you may want to offer fruit juices or decaffeinated drinks.

Breakfast—Serve milk and orange juice. Purchase donuts in the morning at a local donut shop or grocery store. (Many grocery stores make their own donuts daily. They are delicious and less expensive.) If you do not have a good place to purchase fresh donuts, you can always get the packaged powder donuts that most kids love.

FAVORS:

The kids will be going home with their nightshirts and toe paintings. Because you have provided so much food and entertainment, the shirts are enough for favors. If you want to add another gift, consider something like lip gloss for the girls or plastic footballs or basketballs for the boys. You can also purchase plastic cups and paint the kids' names on them. Let the kids use the cups throughout the party and take them home as well.

* 22 *

Girl Time

It's Girl Time! This is a feminine party full of games and crafts just for girls. They will make hair bows and fix their hair, then play a makeup game to get all dolled up. A girl trivia game and cookie bake-off will be followed by a short lesson on true beauty from First Peter 3.

➡ **Suggested Size:** 5 to 12 girls
Suggested Time of Day: afternoon or evening
Type: all girls

YOU WILL NEED:

- Barrettes
- Ribbons
- Wire
- Makeup and nail polish
- Poster boards
- Refreshments
- Cookie sheets
- Ingredients for cookies

INVITATIONS:

Make invitations in the form of a note to a friend. Use pink stationery or paper to make the invitation. Let your daughter write the following information:

IT'S GIRL TIME!!

Dear _____,

I'm having a "get-together" to celebrate my _____ birthday. We're going to make hair bows and play some fantastic games. We'll also have a cookie bake-off.

It will be a blast!

_____
(Date and time)
_____
(Address)

Hope you can come.

Give me a call to RSVP _____.

Love Ya,

Decorate the paper with stickers, stamps, or small drawings. You can buy stickers with fun things like hair accessories, telephones, and flowers. A cute way to seal the envelope would be to put a lipstick kiss on the back.

DECORATIONS:

On the front door hang a welcome sign decorated with lipstick kisses. Use a white or light-colored poster board and write *Welcome* in the center, then apply lipstick to your lips and kiss away. Pink balloons and flowers will give the party a feminine touch.

SCHEDULE: 2 hours

20 minutes—Arrive, talk, make hair bows
30 minutes—Games
25 minutes—Bake cookies
15 minutes—Eat and talk
30 minutes—Girl time trivia

ACTIVITIES:

1. Arrive, talk, make hair bows

As your guests arrive, offer them some drinks and munchies. Let them talk for a little while. When most of the girls arrive, show them how to make hair bows. I will give you basic instructions, but I suggest that you also check out a book titled *Braids and Bows* by Klutz Press. The book has a multitude of hair bow ideas and simple instructions for making them. You will need lots of ribbon, wire, and barrettes. Provide netting material and other creative items to make a variety of bows. Many unusual items are used to make bows these days—everything from balloons to drinking straws. You could also make headbands.

Here is a simple instruction for a loop bow.

You will need about 2 feet of wire, 1 yard of ribbon, and a barrette. Fold the wire in half and knot it through the end of the barrette. Start about 1 inch from the end of the ribbon and wrap the wire around the ribbon to attach it to the barrette. It's ok if the ribbon gets a little scrunched up. Make loops with the ribbon, securing them to the barrette with the wire. After attaching all of the ribbon, tuck the end of the wire under the wire wraps and trim. You can keep the ends of the ribbon from fraying by putting clear nail polish on the ends.

Decorate the ribbon with paints. Let the girls make several bows if you have enough materials.

2. Games

Here are a variety of games created just for girls!

Makeup game—Make a square spinner using poster board and put a brad through the center. Draw four sections on the spinner and label them *eyes, lips, fingernails,* and *cheeks.* Give each girl a chance to spin. If she lands on *eyes,* she applies eye shadow to one eye. If she spins *lips,* she puts lipstick on either her upper lip or her lower lip. For the *nails* she can paint one hand, and for the *cheeks* she can put blush on one cheek. If a girl spins *eyes* and she has already completed her eye makeup, then she skips her turn. The object of the game is to be the first girl to have all of her makeup and nails complete.

If you have more than eight girls at the party, you may want to have two games going at once. Another fun idea is to invite a makeup sales representative to come and help apply the makeup for the girls.

Triple Telephone—Take the traditional telephone game and add a little more challenge. In the traditional game, one girl whispers a message to the girl next to her and the message is passed around the circle until it comes back to the original girl. In triple telephone, instead of passing around one message, choose three girls to start three different messages. The messages do not all have to go in the same direction.

Vary the game even more by having the girls number off, "one, two, one, two." Each girl with the number "one" will start a message to the number "two" on her right. Many messages will be passed at once. The messages go around the entire circle until they return to the originators. The girls then tell their messages in both the original and the altered versions. Use the outcome as an opportunity to teach the girls how dangerous gossip can be and how stories can change so quickly.

Correction, please—Here's another circle game! The object of this game is to pass a sentence out loud, from person to person, changing one word each time. The first person begins with a simple sentence, for example, "The children went to the zoo." The next person responds by changing one word like this, "I beg your pardon, but the mouse went to the zoo." The next person can change another word, and so on around the circle. Allow only a few seconds for the next girl to respond. Have a time limit and encourage unusual and silly word combinations. At the end of the game, point out that one word can make a lot of difference. Tell the girls to be careful what they say, especially if they are telling a story about another person.

3. Bake cookies

Have the ingredients ready for baking several kinds of favorite cookies. Divide the girls into groups to make the cookies, and turn the activity into a contest to make the best cookie creations. Here's a fun way to divide the girls into teams. Put several different colors of M&Ms in a brown paper bag. Let the girls reach in and pick out a candy. The color she picks will determine her cooking group. She will join with all of the others who chose the same color. Encourage all of the girls to participate in adding the ingredients and mixing. The smaller the groups, the better.

If the party takes place around a holiday, you can make cut-out sugar cookies and let the girls decorate them. If you do not have enough oven space, bake them in shifts or ask a neighbor if you can borrow her oven.

While you are waiting for all of the cookies to bake, ask the girls to sit down while you talk to them for a moment. Tell them that they all look lovely with their hair done and makeup on. Ask:

Did you know that the Bible tells us that our beauty should not just come from the outside. First Peter 3:3–4 says, "Do not let your adornment be merely outward—arranging the hair, wearing gold, or putting on fine apparel—rather let it be the hidden person of the heart, with the incorruptible beauty of a gentle and quiet spirit, which is very precious in the sight of God."

We should not depend on makeup and hairstyle for our beauty. The Bible says that our beauty should come from the inside. Our beauty should lie in a gentle and quiet spirit. The verse didn't tell us that we should not wear makeup or pretty hair styles, but it does tell us not to let that be where our beauty comes from.

How can you be beautiful on the inside?

Give the girls some time to discuss ways to develop inward beauty. You may want to assign another adult to watch the cookies in the oven while you are involved with the discussion.

4. Eat and talk

Now take time to eat the cookie creations, talk, and open presents.

5. Girl time trivia

If you have time at the end, play girl-time trivia. It is a simple game that's a young version of the regular trivia games. You can make a game board from poster board and let the girls move game pieces, or you can just play by reading the questions out loud. Play in teams or individually. Enlist your daughter's help to make up the questions. Think of trivia questions that pertain to school, famous singers, and popular TV shows or movies. Stay away from derogatory questions and try to keep them in the areas that most of your guests will know. Here are some sample questions.

- What is the name of the actor who plays _(character name)_ on _(TV show)_?
- Which brown-haired boy has a locker at the corner of Halls A and B?
- What is the name of the quarterback of the school football team?
- Name the three subjects that Mrs. Thompson teaches at school.
- Name two of the novels that are studied in sixth grade English class.

Get the idea? You may want to give prizes for the winning team or for individual correct answers.

FOOD:

You can serve snacks at the beginning of the party or just serve the contest cookies.

Finger sandwiches
Crackers and cheese
Fruit slices
Cookies—Provide ingredients for several kinds of cookies—chocolate chip, peanut butter, M&Ms, oatmeal, or sugar cookies.

FAVORS:

1. Hair bows
2. Bag of cookies
3. Young girl's perfume or lip gloss
4. Mirror and comb set
5. Stationery and pen
6. Frame or bookmark with 1 Peter 3:3–4 written on it

* 23 *

Fiesta Mexico!

Tacos, enchiladas, tamales! The food will be great, especially after some Mexican games and a little Spanish lesson. This will make a perfect dinner party for both the señores and señoritas. The biblical emphasis will be on John 3:16 (in Spanish) and a prayer for our missionaries in Mexico. Youth groups may enjoy this party as a way to be introduced to a missionary or a missions trip or just an opportunity to get together.

➡️ **Suggested Size:** 8 to 15 kids
Suggested Time of Day: evening
Type: boys, girls, or both

YOU WILL NEED:

- Bright colored poster boards
- Newspaper, flour, paint
- Balls
- Chapete ball or Hacky Sack
- Mexican food
- Items from Mexico

INVITATIONS:

There is usually a plentiful supply of Mexican party invitations at party stores or card shops, but your homemade invitations will be more personal and inviting. Cut out sombreros from colored poster board. Use very bright, even fluorescent, colors. On the front, write the Mexican greeting *Hóla!* On the back you will write the pertinent information about the party. If you want your guests to dress in Mexican attire, be sure to indicate that on your invitation.

JOIN US FOR A FANTASTIC FIESTA!

The Mexican fun begins at _____ (time)

On: _____ (date)

Location: _____ (address)

RSVP: _____ (name and phone number)

DECORATIONS:

Your theme colors will be bright colors such as pink, orange, yellow, and turquoise. Buy lots of streamers and balloons in these colors. Piñatas will make festive decorations. Party stores usually carry them or you can make your own. Use crumpled newspaper to make any shape you desire and tape it to help it stay together. Next, use strips of newspaper dipped in a thin paste made of flour and water to cover the object. Overlap the strips of newspaper to make sure you have covered the entire piñata. Let it dry for forty-eight hours and then paint it as you desire with tempera paint. Hang some piñatas from the ceiling in the main rooms for the party.

At each table use Mexican paraphernalia as center pieces. Sombreros filled with chips make great decorations or center pieces. You may be able to find some Mexican flags and maracas at a party store. Ask some of your friends who have been to Mexico to lend to you any items that they may have.

Place a sombrero or piñata on the front door with a small sign that says *Hóla!* Check at a music store to see if you can find any tapes of Mexican music. As the guests arrive, have the music playing to set a fiesta mood.

SCHEDULE: 2 hours

10 minutes—Arrive, talk, snack
25 minutes—Game one, Indian kickball
20 minutes—Game two, Chapete
40 minutes—Eat!
25 minutes—Spanish lesson

ACTIVITIES:

1. Arrive, talk, snack

Greet your guests at the door with a greeting such as *Hóla!* or *Buenos dias!* Encourage them to mingle and eat while the rest of the kids arrive. Place tortilla chips and salsa around the room and assign someone to help serve soft drinks. Here are some games to play as you wait for all the guests to arrive.

Sombrero toss—Set out a large basket or box, mark a line several yards away, and have kids try to toss the hat into the basket or box.

Mexican bean pitch—Give everyone a large dried bean. Each player will mark his bean with a paint pen or marker to be able to identify his bean. The object of the game is to try to pitch your bean as close to a line as possible without going over. Use masking tape to make the line and have players stand several feet away. The person whose bean is on the line or closest to it is the winner. Play several rounds of this game.

Soccer—Active guests may want to kick around a soccer ball in the yard during this time.

Game One—After most of the guests have arrived, ask them to gather in one main room to explain the game. The first game is Indian kickball, which originated with the Tarahumara Indians of Mexico. This particular race was once a celebrated annual event among the Indians and was a very difficult race covering twenty to thirty miles: but don't worry, we will scale it down considerably.

Form at least two teams of three to six players per team. Have each participant draw a number from a basket to determine which team she will be on. If you are planning to have three teams, then put the numbers one, two, and three in the basket for everyone to draw. Make sure the teams are the same size.

Although the Indians used a stone or a root cut from a tree, your teams will be using a ball. Still, the ball should be one that is small and cannot be kicked long distances easily. You can use a small ball made of crumpled tin foil or crumpled newspaper held together with masking tape.

Establish a course for the race ahead of time, anywhere between a hundred yards and a half mile. The course can run through your neighborhood, around your house, or in a nearby field. Stay away from areas where there could be traffic, and avoid crossing streets. You may want to walk it through with the teams to establish any guidelines. Make sure you have a specific start and finish. The game is played by the entire team working together to get its ball across the finish. One team member kicks the ball and then moves out of the way for another member on his team to kick. That member kicks, then moves out of the way for another of his team members to kick, all the while moving the ball closer to the finish line. No particular order needs to be followed; just make sure that no team member kicks the ball twice in a row.

Each team should be accompanied by an adult or referee to make sure that they play fair and that no one kicks the ball twice in a row. If the ball is kicked twice by the same player, the team must return to the starting line. The first team to kick the ball across the finish line wins!

Prizes for the winning team can be a pack of chewing gum or candy. The kids may want to play this game several times. They will get better and better with each try once they get the hang of it.

This game is an outdoor game. If the weather is bad you could scale it down and play in the basement or another large room in the house. Move the furniture out of the play zone.

Game Two—Chapete is a game that has been played for centuries among Mexican teenagers and young adults. Chapete is a very active and athletic game, although you don't actually move anywhere. It has been marketed by a toy company under the name of *Hacky Sack*. For the game you can purchase several Hacky Sack balls or make your own by sewing a piece of leather or thick cloth filled with beans, sand, or rice. Or, you could play the game with a crumpled-up piece of foil.

You may want to form new teams of about four to six players by drawing numbers or colors. The rules are simple: just keep the little ball in the air using your feet, knees, or thighs, but no hands. Players stand in a circle and launch the ball into play. Keep score by the number of hits the ball receives before it hits the ground. Try not to kick the other players by mistake! There's no need for prizes or awards for this game; it's just plain fun. The groups can compete between themselves by trying to get the most hits before the ball hits the ground.

Do not be surprised if the kids do not seem to be able to do this game very well. This game requires skill and practice. The kids will have fun just trying to keep the ball in the air. You may want to let them start out with a balloon to practice and then let them try the small ball.

Basketball has its early roots with the ancient Mayan culture. If it is nice outside, play basketball with a regular ball. If you do not have a basketball hoop available, use laundry baskets at both ends of the court. This will present some different challenges in getting the ball into the basket.

If you have bad weather, use a sponge basketball or a balloon. Use a room that has a large amount of open space; move furniture if you need to. Put a laundry basket or a hoop at both ends of the room.

Have all the players sit on the floor. Divide into teams by counting off. The players can shoot or pass the ball from anywhere to each other, trying to get it to the teammate closest to their basket. The opposing team members can try to intercept shots as long as there is no physical contact. Give free shots when fouls occur. Have a referee at each end of the room to retrieve stray balls and throw them back to the players. After a team makes a basket, the ball goes to the other team.

2. Eat!

Gather everyone together, say a blessing, and then chow down. It may be best to serve buffet style and let everyone sit in the living room, on the couch, and on the floor instead of at tables.

3. Spanish lesson

If you have a friend who speaks Spanish or if you know of a missionary to Mexico who is in the area, ask her to help with this part of the party. You can handle this part by yourself even if you have never learned any Spanish. Check with a local school to ask a Spanish teacher to help you pronounce the words correctly. You could even use a tape recording of someone who is well versed in the Spanish language.

Begin by asking the kids if any of them knows some Spanish words. Hold up cards with the Spanish words from the list below. Ask them if they know how to pronounce the word or let them have fun guessing how to pronounce it. Next let them attempt to guess the meaning of the word. Give some hints if they need them. This time is meant to be a fun, not a serious lesson.

Here are some words to write on the cards.

- *las panques* (pancakes)
- *los lonches* (sandwiches)
- *el helado* (ice cream)
- *la sirvilleta* (the napkin)
- *la leche* (milk)
- *la pierna* (the leg)

- *la cabeza* (the head)
- *los ojos* (the eyes)
- *el brazo* (the arm)
- *la ventana* (the window)

Next, bring out a poster with the words of John 3:16 written in Spanish. Do not let them see the reference and ask them if they can guess what the poster says. Once they have figured out that this is John 3:16, try to read the verse as a group. Have fun with this and don't worry about pronouncing every word perfectly.

Juan 3:16
Porque de tal manera amó Dios al mundo, que dio a su hijo unigénito, para que todos los que en él crean no se pierdan más tengan vida eterna.

At this time you may want to briefly tell about missionaries in Mexico that your church supports. Ask the kids to pray with you for these missionaries and for the good news about Jesus to spread to every country.

FOOD:

This is a fairly simple menu, but you may want to ask several cohosts to help bring some of the food. You could make this a Mexican pot-luck dinner and ask every guest to bring a dish. If you do, don't forget to include that request on the invitation.

Chicken enchiladas—See recipe below.
Make-your-own tacos—Prepare taco meat using ground beef and a
    package of taco seasoning. Offer soft or hard tortillas, cheese, and
    chopped lettuce and tomatoes.
Tamales—You can purchase frozen and canned tamales at most gro-
    cery stores.
Refried beans and spanish rice
Fresh fruit—Apples, oranges, and sliced avocados.
Chips, bean dip, and salsa
Lemonade or soft drinks
Sopaipillas or Pecan Praline Ice Cream—Recipe for sopaipillas below.

Sour Cream Chicken Enchiladas

1 dozen flour tortillas
1 small chicken (cooked, boned, and chopped)
1½ cups chicken stock
1½ cups grated cheddar cheese
1 medium onion, chopped
1 cup grated Monterey Jack cheese
1 can chopped green chilis
1 can cream of chicken soup
1 cup sour cream

Mix together chopped chicken, onion, and cheddar cheese. Soften tortillas by steaming. Put chicken mixture in tortillas, 1 to 2 tablespoons full per tortilla, and roll tightly. Place in a greased 9" x 13" baking dish. Combine chicken soup, chicken stock, sour cream, and green chilis. Pour over enchiladas and bake at 350° for 30 minutes. Sprinkle Monterey Jack cheese on top and bake again until cheese melts.

Sopaipillas

Sift together 4 cups sifted flour, 1½ teaspoons salt, 1 tablespoon baking powder, and 3 tablespoons sugar. Cut in ¼ cup shortening until mixture is texture of coarse meal. Add enough water so dough holds together. Chill 15 minutes. Roll out ¼ inch thick. Cut into 1½ inch squares. Deep fry in oil, heated to 390°, until puffed and golden. Drain on paper towels. While hot, sprinkle with cinnamon sugar and serve with honey.

FAVORS:

1. Copies of John 3:16 in Spanish—Encourage the kids to continue to practice and remember it.
2. Small Mexican flag
3. Miniature piñatas
4. Mexican paper flowers

Party Variation:

You can change the focus of this party from Mexico to another country such as China or Russia. The library is a good resource for information on international games and foods.

* 24 *

Unexpected Event

Surprise parties are always fun, especially if the guests are the ones being surprised. Send party information to the parents of the guests instructing them to have their children prepared. The date and event will remain a secret to the kids. At the appointed hour, the guests will be picked up for the party. The theme comes from Matthew 24:36–44, which says concerning the coming of the Son of Man, "But of that day and hour no one knows."

➡ Suggested Size:	5 to 12 kids
Suggested Time of Day:	morning, afternoon, or evening The time of day that you choose is a decision that is totally up to you. I personally think a breakfast party is a load of fun, but I suggest that you start at about 9:30 A.M. Not everyone is a morning person, and they may not be thrilled with early morning surprise visitors.
Type:	all boys or all girls

YOU WILL NEED:

- Stationery
- Food or money for a restaurant
- Crepe paper and balloons

INVITATIONS:

Mail invitations to the parents instead of the kids since you want the kids to be surprised when they are picked up for the party. Write the invitations on regular stationery so as not to arouse suspicion. The idea is to make sure the parents have the kids ready without telling them about the party. The invitation should read something like this:

SHH! SHH!

Your daughter [or son] is invited to an unexpected party!
Have your child at home and dressed (casual)
on _____ (date) _____.
We will pick her/him up at _____ (time) _____
and return at _____.
Please keep this hush-hush because we want it to be a surprise for everyone.
Your RSVP is very important.

Sincerely,

You may want to add information about the meal or the location of the party, although they can obtain this information when they RSVP. You can also include any birthday information that may apply.

DECORATIONS:

Start off by decorating the car. Attach crepe paper streamers to the antenna, mirrors, and fender. Write the word *surprise* on the windows using white shoe polish. Attach some balloons to the outside of the car too.

The rest of the decorations depend on whether you take the kids to a restaurant or back to your house to eat. At a restaurant you may want to have a bunch of helium balloons at the table where you sit. If you go home, you will need balloons and paper goods. I suggest you choose two or three theme colors for the balloons, streamers, and paper items. Let your son or daughter choose his or her favorite colors.

SCHEDULE: 2 hours or more

20 to 50 minutes—Gather the guests
60 minutes—Eat and talk
40 minutes—Party activity
20 to 50 minutes—Take guests home

ACTIVITIES:

1. Gather the guests

Call anyone who did not RSVP to see if their kids will be there. If you catch someone totally off guard when you are picking them up, especially in the morning, allow them about three minutes to get themselves ready. Hopefully this will not happen because the parents are supposed to have their child ready, but you never know what can happen. Be sure that you have enough seats and seat belts for everyone. Ask other parents to help with transportation. If you are going to a restaurant, call ahead and reserve a table for your group.

Map out your route so that you do not waste time crisscrossing from one side of town to the other. Give each driver addresses that are in the same vicinity. Notice that I allowed 20 to 50 minutes for gathering the guests. The time you'll spend depends on how far apart your guests live.

2. Eat and talk

After the kids have chowed down on a great meal, ask them if they enjoyed being surprised. You will find that some loved it and others didn't like the element of surprise. Ask the kids if they realize that the Bible says that Jesus will return one day. Tell them that it also says that we do not know the day or the hour, only God knows. Then say, "God does tell us to be ready for His coming, even though we do not know the day or time. He will gather us together with Him in the clouds. What a glorious day that will be!"

Read Matthew 24:31,36–44 to the group to give them a clearer picture of Jesus' return. Use this opportunity to tell the group that it is only those who have believed in Jesus who will be gathered to Him. Ask the kids how they can be prepared for the return of Jesus.

3. Party activity

Plan a game or activity for the kids to release some energy. This is optional. The meal and discussion may be enough for the party. Here are some suggestions for fun games for either guys or gals just in case.

Backseat Drivers—You will need some open space for this game. Divide the group into pairs by telling each guest to stand in a circle and put one of his hands in the middle. Grab two hands out of the pile to form a pair. That pair moves outside the circle and you grab two more until all pairs have been formed.

Now, one player acts as the car and the other is the driver. Cars hold their hands out in front (imitating headlights) and close their eyes. You can use blindfolds if you like. The drivers keep their eyes open and steer cars by standing behind and placing their hands on their partner's shoulders. One car and driver are chosen to be "It." They will try to tag the other cars. Drivers carefully maneuver cars around other cars trying to avoid getting tagged. Speeding is not allowed. When a car is tagged, that becomes It. Cars and drivers switch roles and the game continues.

The Great Pipeline—Give each player a 9-inch by 12-inch sheet of construction paper and two paper clips for each player. You will also need two small balls made from crumpled paper or foil. Tell the players to roll their papers into cylinders and fasten with paper clips.

Separate the players into two teams by counting off. Have them stand in two parallel lines and tell them to hold their paper cylinders end to end to create a long pipe. When you give the signal, the first player on each team will drop the ball into the end of their pipe. The team members must jiggle the balls from one cylinder to the next. If the ball drops on the floor, the last person to have the ball must pick it up and try again. When the ball gets to the end, then it is passed back to the start again. The first team to get the ball back to the start wins.

Force field—Tie a rope from one side of the room to the other to divide the room in half. The rope should be about three feet off the floor. Gather everyone on one side of the rope. From the rope to the floor will be an electric force field. Players who accidentally touch it are zapped with electricity and must fall to the floor and remain there for the rest of the game.

The object of the game is to get everyone from one side of the rope to the other without getting zapped. The problem requires group cooperation. Players cannot go under the rope or try to jump the height, but must work together to lift each other carefully over the force field. Only one object can be used to help, such as a chair or desk or small table. Be careful that players do not throw each other over the force field and that the last person doesn't dive over it. Another way to play the game is to get over the force field in total silence as if it were a secret escape. Players will have to communicate with hand motions.

Here are some other optional ideas to do with the kids after eating. Take them to the local recreation center to play basketball or let them play some flag football in the yard. You could also take them to a field to play soccer or kickball. Bowling is another option.

Or take the kids to a gym where they can practice gymnastics and tumbling. At home, you could move furniture to create a large open space to let them practice some tumbling. Ask a high school student, who has experience in tumbling or cheerleading, to come and lead the kids in some exercise. Other options include dancing, listening to music, playing a fun board game, or roller skating.

4. Take guests home

Return the kids to their homes in the same organized manner that you picked them up. Remind them as you drop them off always to be ready for the time when Jesus comes back.

FOOD:

Breakfast
   Pancakes
   Eggs
   Sausage
   Juice
Lunch or dinner
   Pizza or hamburgers
   Fruit and chips
   Soft drinks
   Cake and ice cream

FAVORS: Pick and choose

1. Date books or calendars
2. Inexpensive watches—At discount stores, you can find digital watches for a great price. You may want to consider this if you have a small group.

3. Pouch purses
4. Key chains—There is such a wide variety of key chains available. Check with your Christian bookstore, discount stores, or party stores.

* 25 *

Movie Critics

Move over Siskel and Ebert, and make room for an insightful group of young critics. Here is an opportunity to discuss and rate some of the latest movies according to God's criteria. After the kids rate the movies, they will watch a good movie, complete with popcorn, candy, and cokes. Our theme will be from Romans 12:2: "And do not be conformed to this world, but be transformed by the renewing of your mind."

➡ **Suggested Size:**   6 to 20 kids
Suggested Time of Day: evening, after dinner
Type: boys, girls, or both

YOU WILL NEED:

- VCR and preselected video
- Poster boards
- Popcorn (lots), candy, soft drinks
- Colored construction paper, glitter, and glue
- Movie guide from newspaper
- Movie posters

INVITATIONS:

Make invitations in the shape of a star. Cut 4-inch stars out of yellow poster board and cover one side with glitter. Your message will read something like this:

Movie critics needed

on _____ (date) _____ .

Showtime is from _____ to _____ :

Theater address _____ (your address) _____

See you at the movies!

Send the stars in a business-size envelope.

Another idea for invitations, if your kids feel daring, is to create a short video to invite the guests. Have several friends work together to write and produce the video. Encourage the kids to dress up and ham it up. Distribute the movie by attaching a list of people to pass it to.

You will want to distribute the video invitation early so that everyone will have a chance to view it. You may want to make three or four identical videos to distribute so that the list of people to pass it to will be shorter. If this party is for the entire youth group, show the video at one of the youth gatherings a few weeks prior to the party.

DECORATIONS:

You will want to give your decorations a movie theater theme. On the front door, take a black poster board and cut a smaller white poster to place in the center. Make this sign look like a theater billboard. Cut out yellow circles and place around the black area to look like marquee lights. Write *Welcome to the Movies* in the center.

See if you can obtain some movie posters from local theaters to hang around the party rooms. Make another billboard poster to write the theme verse, Romans 12:2.

Play the soundtrack to a recent movie for background music as the kids arrive. Your son or daughter should be able to help you decide which soundtrack to choose.

SCHEDULE: about 2½ hours

20 minutes—Arrive, make Hollywood glasses
30 minutes—Gather, break into groups, critique movies
1½ hours—Refreshments and video

ACTIVITIES:

1. Arrive, make Hollywood glasses

As the guests arrive, greet them at the door and hand them a colored ticket. Use the tickets later to separate the kids into critique groups. Before the party, prepare several different colors of tickets that look similar to movie tickets. The kids will group with the others who have the same ticket color.

Ask an assistant to help serve soft drinks as the guests arrive and mingle. Make a stencil using a pair of glasses and trace around them. Lean them on their side in order to trace the arms. The kids will make their own star-studded Hollywood glasses during the arrival time. Provide black poster board, stencil, glitter, sequins, glue, and scissors. Let the kids trace the stencil and cut out their own glasses, then decorate them with glitter and sequins. Put newspaper under the work area since glitter tends to get everywhere. Add color plastic or cellophane to make the lenses.

Here is an acting game to play if there is time.

Major transformations—Divide the group into two teams by counting off. The object of the game is for the players to form as quickly as possible into whatever object you describe. Call out the name of an object, and the team members must arrange themselves into that shape. If you say "jumbo jet," then the players must decide who will be the wings, the cockpit, the body, and the tail. Other ideas for transformations are a forest, a ship, a bunch of balloons, a house, a church, and a bus. The teams compete to be the first finished with the best representation. You be the judge.

2. Critique movies

After making the glasses or playing the game, tell the kids to find the others who have the same color ticket that they do. Make sure the groups are close or equal in size. Give each group a critique sheet like the one found at the end of this chapter, along with a pencil and a movie information sheet. In order to critique the movie, you will need to give each group an information sheet about a different movie. To make your information sheets, cut out advertisements for current movies from the newspaper and glue them to construction paper. On the other side of the construction paper compile all the information that you can gather about the movie. You will want to include the ratings and a brief summary of the plot, without being too detailed. Gather your information from newspaper reviews and from people you know who have seen the movies. Use current, popular movies, not necessarily good movies.

Each group will read its information sheet, critique the movie according to God's standards, and then give the movie a rating. Allow the groups to work for about 25 to 30 minutes, then stop and discuss the outcomes of the critiques. Their conclusions should be based on Romans 12:2. See page 187.

Tell the kids that as they decide what they are going to put into their minds, they should consider God's criteria. Remind the kids that what they put into their minds stays there and becomes evident in their actions. Garbage in, garbage out. Encourage the kids to think it through before they subject their minds to certain movies that may not be glorifying to God.

3. Refreshments and video

Now it's show time! Invite everyone to the dining room to load up on refreshments before the movie begins. Make your dining room table look like a concession stand. On a poster, list the items available (leave out prices). Serve popcorn in small brown paper bags or large cups. Lay out the candy so that all the selections are visible. You may want to tell them to take just one of each item.

After everyone has collected their goodies, ask them to find a seat in the den, then start the video. Be sure that the movie you have chosen is one that fits God's criteria. You will want to give the kids a good example of a movie that is enjoyable as well as pleasing to God. Here is the address of a Christian organization that monitors movies and publishes the information in a monthly newsletter. This organization is an excellent resource for discovering good, God-pleasing movies.

Movie Morality Ministries
1309 Seminole Dr.
Richardson, TX 75080-3736
214-231-9910

FOOD:

Soft drinks—Make sure you have plenty of drinks on hand since you will be serving drinks at the beginning of the party and during the movie. Buy three or four 2-liter bottles for every ten kids.

Popcorn—Make your own popcorn or buy some giant bags of prepopped popcorn from the grocery store.

Candy—Select candy that you usually see at the movie theater concession stand. Buy candy by the box to save money.

FAVORS:

1. Gift certificates to the concession stand at a local movie theater
2. Dollar movie passes
3. Gift certificates to a video store
4. Sunglasses or homemade Hollywood glasses
5. Movie posters or other items with movie logos
6. Cup or mug with star shapes and each person's name painted on
7. Cap with painted stars or star studs

God's Movie Criteria
(see Romans 12:2)

Rate your movie in each area on a scale of 1 to 5. Five represents being totally in line with God's Word and 1 represents being in line with the world's philosophy.

	THE WORLD SAYS:	GOD SAYS:
———1. Language:	Freedom of speech	Eph. 4:29 Let no corrupt word proceed out of your mouth.
———2. Treatment of Enemies:	Revenge	Rom. 12:17 Repay no one evil for evil.
———3. Sex:	Anything goes	1 Cor. 6:18 Flee sexual immorality.
———4. Honesty:	Tell the truth if . . .	Col. 3:9 Do not lie.

How would you rate this movie?
PG—Pleases God: 20 points
LW—Lukewarm: 9 to 19 points
A—Abomination to the Lord: 4 to 8 points

Other aspects you can add into the grading are: supernatural power, obedience, and love of money.

* 26 *

Sports Spectacular

Choose your sport: basketball, football, baseball, or hockey! Get the guys or girls together to eat and watch the game, or take the kids to a local event. If they watch a game on TV, then they will have fun-filled competitions during the commercial breaks and at halftime. The theme from the Bible is Hebrews 12:1–2: We are surrounded by witnesses watching us run in the game of life.

➡ **Suggested Size:**	5 to 20, (3 to 8 if you are going to a game)
Suggested Time of Day:	Game time
Type:	All boys (this could also work for sports-minded girls)

YOU WILL NEED:

- TV or tickets to a local game
- Poster board
- Snacks
- Items for competitions

INVITATIONS:

If you are going to watch the game on TV, make invitations in the shape of a TV. If you are going to the game, make the invitations in the shape of a ticket. Use poster board to cut the shapes and display the information as you see below.

We're getting together to watch
the _____ game!
Game starts at: _____ (time and date) _____
Address: _____
RSVP: _____

or

Let's go to the _____ game!
Meet at: _____ (address) _____
On: _____ (date) _____
At: _____ (time) _____ sharp!
RSVP: _____

SCHEDULE:

The schedule for this party is to watch the game and have small competitions during the commercial breaks. If you choose to go to a game, have dessert together afterward so that you can have a chance to talk.

ACTIVITIES:

1. Watch the game on TV

Invite the kids to arrive right when the game starts. Provide plenty of snacks and drinks to consume while watching the game. Here are some simple competitions to hold during the breaks:

Finger football—Make a small 1-inch ball using aluminum foil or folded paper. Let the boys compete against each other as they use their fingers to maneuver the ball. Let the boys try to flick the ball with their fingers to kick a goal. Tape straws together to make goal posts.

Sports trivia contest—Locate sports trivia cards or make your own. Read questions aloud and let the boys earn points by being the first one to answer correctly. At the end of the party, give a prize to the person who accumulated the most points. You can have an ongoing trivia game throughout the party.

The real thing—During halftime go outside and play the real thing. Or play inside the house with a sponge ball and one handicap: the boys must play on their knees. Move furniture if necessary.

Arm wrestling—Hold a tournament.

Punt, pass, and kick competitions—Go outdoors and hold the competition in the front yard or use sponge balls inside. You can have free throw competition for basketball; pitch and hit for baseball, and so on.

Golf putting competition—You will need a putter, a coffee can, and a golf ball. Let the boys attempt to putt the ball into the can. Give prizes to those who are successful.

Bloopers—Rent a sports blooper video that you can watch during some of the commercial breaks.

Tug-of-war—Get a rope, divide into teams and play tug-of-war.

Crab soccer—Clear away the furniture and play Crab soccer using a balloon. In Crab soccer the players play on their hands and feet, the front of their bodies upward. Shoes off for this game.

2. Dessert and discussion

At the end of the game, let the boys make their own sundaes. As they are eating their creations, ask them to listen up. Let this be a casual discussion time and not a sermon. Read Hebrews 12:1–2 and say:

These verses tell us that we are surrounded by a great cloud of spectators, as if we are running in a race. It tells us to take off every weight and the sin that ensnares us. Runners wear as little as possible, so that they will not be slowed down when they run. We must lay aside the things in life that keep us from following God. What are some of those things?

Give the boys an opportunity to answer. Remind them that in this race of life, we are to keep our eyes on Jesus, just as a runner keeps his eye on the finish line.

FOOD:

Submarine sandwiches
Chips, pretzels, and popcorn
Grapes and fruit slices
Soft drinks—Buy three 2-liter bottles for every five guests.
Sundaes—Make your own sundaes with a variety of ice cream and
toppings.

FAVORS:

1. Football or baseball cards—Athletes in Action provides cards
   with local athletes' testimonies on the back. Check your local
   phone directory for the Athletes in Action chapter nearest you.
2. Local sports paraphernalia—Buttons, pennants, caps, etc.
3. Small plastic footballs, basketballs, or soccer balls

* 27 *

Mall Madness

Get together at one of the kids' favorite hangouts: the mall! Invite everyone to meet at a specific location in the mall for an incredible scavenger hunt. Small groups will scurry through the mall gathering the items on their lists. The party will end with snacks and a talk about God's values versus the world's. The theme verses will be Matthew 6:19–20: "Do not lay up for yourselves treasures on earth . . . but lay up for yourselves treasures in heaven." This is an easy party to give because it requires minimal preparation.

➡ **Suggested Size:** 10 to 25
Suggested Time of Day: afternoon or evening
Type: all girls, all boys, or mixed

YOU WILL NEED:

- Scavenger hunt list
- Snacks and beverages
- Sacks
- Twine or ribbon

INVITATIONS:

If you are inviting fifteen people or fewer, make invitations in the form of shopping bags. Using brown paper grocery bags or solid color wrapping paper, cut 3½-inch by 4-inch rectangles. Glue two rectangles together on the sides and bottom, leaving the top open. Tape twine or ribbon to the top to create handles. On the side of the bag, write a fictitious store name such as *Betty's Boutique* for the girls' invitations or *Fred's Sporting Goods* for the boys'. Write the information for the party on a plain index card and stick it in the top of the little bag.

```
┌─────────────────────────────────────────────────────────┐
│                   IT'S MALL MADNESS!                      │
│                                                           │
│  Meet us at the mall for an incredibly fun scavenger hunt.│
│  _____     │
│                       (date, time)                        │
│  _____     │
│                     (exact location)                      │
│  RSVP _____      │
│                    (name and number)                      │
│                    DON'T BE LATE!!                         │
└─────────────────────────────────────────────────────────┘
```

You will want to choose a location in the mall that is easy to find and is good for meeting. Most malls have several areas with benches or other places to sit. Be specific on the invitation; for example, write "We will gather at the benches in front of Susie's Footwear on the lower level near Biggs Department Store.

If you are inviting more than fifteen people, make an invitation that you can have photocopied on colored paper. Write the same information on the invitation and draw small shopping bags in the four corners.

DECORATIONS:

You will need only a few decorations since most of the party will take place at the mall. To decorate at home, purchase some large brightly colored gift bags or use some shopping bags that you may already have from some of the major department stores. Put colored tissue paper in the bags so that it shows out of the top. Distribute bags around the house. You may want to even attach a bag to the front door with the word *Welcome* written across the front.

Limit the colors that you decorate with to about three or so and use one of those colors for your paper plate and napkins selections. You may want to have a few balloons to mark the place where you gather at the mall. Use regular party name tags.

SCHEDULE: 2 hours

10 minutes—Meet and talk
10 minutes—Divide into groups, go over rules

60 minutes—Scavenger hunt
40 minutes—Regroup, go to house, snacks, and talk

ACTIVITIES:

1. Meet and talk

As you gather at the mall, be sure to greet everyone as he arrives and give him a name tag. Encourage everyone to stay together because you will be starting soon. Have a large bag of popcorn for the kids to munch on as they wait for the rest of the kids to arrive.

2. Divide into groups, go over rules

After most of the kids have arrived, gather them together so that you can explain the rules. Tell them they will be breaking into groups and there will be an adult with each group. Several weeks before the party, you will need to ask some adult friends or other parents to assist in leading the groups. The leader will go with her group as they search for the different items on the scavanger hunt list.

There are several rules that you will want to make very clear to the kids before you begin.

- No running. Stress the importance of kind and decent behavior at the mall.
- Listen to and respect your group leader.
- Return in exactly one hour to the same location in the mall. Any group that is late will have points taken away from their score.
- Do not leave the mall.
- Do not take anything without asking first.
- Have an incredibly fun time!!

Remind the kids that they may not be able to find all the items on the list. The object of the game is to be the group that finds the most items or has the highest score.

In order to be fair in dividing into groups, write down everyone's name and put it in a hat. Have each group leader pick names out of the hat for his or her group. The number in each group will be determined by how many group leaders you have and how many kids you have in attendance. A nice size group would be five or six people.

After the groups have been formed, let each group determine a team name. Be sure to synchronize watches and announce the exact time

everyone must return. Hand each group leader the scavenger hunt list
and a bag to collect the items.

3. Scavenger hunt

Your scavenger hunt list can be as long and as difficult as you want.
Use the list provided or make up your own list using specific names of
stores in your mall. You may choose to give a point value to the items
so that some of the "harder to find" items have a higher point value.
Another variation of the scavenger hunt that does not require a list is
to tell each group to collect twenty-six items, one that starts with each
letter of the alphabet. If you use this option, you may want to substi-
tute *ch* and *sh* for *X* and *Z*.

Another variation is a Polaroid scavenger hunt where each team is
given a camera and a list of scenes to photograph.

Mall Scavenger Hunt

10 points	The signature of a tie salesman under twenty-five years old
15 points	The lid of a shoe box
10 points	The smallest sack from a major department store
10 points	A green gum wrapper
10 points	The ring size of the top salesman at a jewelry store
5 points	One half-eaten french fry
10 points	A straw with a blue stripe
20 points	A hanger given to you by the tallest salesperson in a clothing store
5 points	Three peanuts or popcorn kernels
10 points	A napkin with a lipstick stain
20 points	A perfume sample that has a name that starts with a vowel
20 points	A free bookmark
10 points	A receipt from the southern-most store in the mall
20 points	A green or white pencil
10 points	A jewelry gift box
10 points	The middle name of the mall security guard
5 points	A red cup

4. Regroup, go to house, snacks, talk

As you gather together again, have each group leave with their group
leader and go to your home. Make sure that the leaders have enough
seat belts to accommodate everyone. You may have to mix some
groups according to how many people can fit into the various cars.

As the kids arrive at your home, allow everyone to get a plate and load up on goodies. Have all the food prepared ahead of time and ready to be set out before you leave for the mall.

Tally the scores from the scavenger hunt while everyone is eating.

After the kids have snacked for a while, get their attention, have them sit down, and announce the winning team. Allow anyone who wants to share a funny experience to do so, and offer prizes for the funniest stories. Lead into the lesson at this time. Tell the kids that the mall is a place that represents things that money can buy; the treasures of this earth. "The Bible says that we are not supposed to lay up for ourselves treasures of this earth."

Have Matthew 6:19–20 written out on a poster board or on the side of a large solid color shopping bag and read them to the group.

Ask, "Does that mean that we should never buy anything for ourselves? Of course not, but what does it mean?" Lead them to discover that we should not make it our sole focus in life to gather more and more possessions for ourselves.

"The Bible goes on to say that we are to lay up treasures in Heaven. What are those? What will last forever? If we invest our lives in these things, we know we will have treasures in heaven."

After the discussion, offer some dessert and let the kids talk until they leave. Don't forget some background music while they mingle.

FOOD:

A variety of snacks will be the perfect food for the kids to munch on as they return to your house. If it is near the dinner hour and you want to have dinner, serve pizza. You can call a pizza delivery service from the mall as you are leaving so that the pizza will arrive soon after you do.

Snacks
  Party mix
  Chips and dip
  Tortillas
  Salsa
Dessert
  Brownies
  Cookies
  Cupcakes
  Soft drinks—Provide three 2-liter bottles for every five kids. You
    may want to ask some of your group leaders to help bring some of
    the snacks if you have a large group attending.

FAVORS:

1. Discount coupons to mall stores—Many times stores will give out percentage discounts if you explain why you need them.
2. Inexpensive wallets—Look for them at party stores and discount stores. Order from the catalog that I recommend in the back of the book.
3. Plastic knickknack or tool boxes—Paint the Bible verse on the side.
4. Souvenirs or promotional items from mall stores—This may take some legwork on your part, but go to the managers of several different stores in the mall, tell them about the party, and ask them if they have any free promotional items. You will be surprised what some stores offer, such as pencils, visors, cups, key chains, etc. See what you can find. Don't forget perfume and cologne samples at the department stores.

* 28 *

Recording Stars

Gather a few tape recorders and get ready for a barrel of fun! Guests will receive a cassette tape with a rap song that invites them to the celebration. At the party they will break into teams and record different sounds that are on their team list. There will be loads of laughs while listening to the recordings. The theme verse is Mark 4:24, "Take heed what you hear."

➡ **Suggested Size:**   8 to 20 kids
  Suggested Time of Day: afternoon or evening
  Type: boys, girls, or both

YOU WILL NEED:

- Several tape recorders
- Cassette tapes
- Snacks and drinks
- Poster board
- List of sounds to record

INVITATIONS:

Purchase short, inexpensive cassette tapes to be used for the invitations. You may want to ask several friends to help in the production of the tape. Use a rap song to present the party information because they are easy and fun to make up (get your kids to help). Here is an example of a rap invitation. You will need to use your own party information to create your rap, but this example can get you started.

Invitation Rap

My name is Karol, and I've got some news,
On Saturday night, you won't be singing the blues.
We're going to get together to have some fun,
So mark your calendar and be sure to come.
The time is 6:30 on October twenty-third.
You better be there or be a nerd.
Everything is happening on Bentwood Trail,
4622; be there and don't fail.
We're going to be recording your voice and mine.
Don't you have a worry, you'll do just fine.
See you there and remember to RSVP,
The number's simple, 249-1523.

DECORATIONS:

Cut out giant stars from yellow poster board and decorate them with glitter. Hang them up around the room. You could make smaller stars, one with each guest's name on it, to decorate the room. Using a black poster board, cut out a giant set of headphones. Write Mark 4:24 on it with a white paint pen or chalk.

SCHEDULE: 2 hours

20 minutes—Arrive, mingle, snacks, game
50 minutes—Explain and record
20 minutes—Talk and eat
30 minutes—Listen to productions and lesson

ACTIVITIES:

1. Arrive, mingle, snacks, game

As you greet your guests at the door, point them in the direction of the soft drinks and chips. You will want to have music by a popular Christian musician playing in the background. A fun game to play as you wait for everyone to arrive is "Name That Tune." Gather several popular tapes and play short segments of songs on the tape recorder. The kids must identify the singer and the title of the song. Make the game more difficult by playing very short segments. Be sure to use familiar artists and songs.

2. Recording game

Ask everyone to join you in the den for an explanation of the game. First you will need to divide up into teams by having each person pick a song title out of a hat. Four or five others will have that same title on their pieces of paper too. When you say "go!" each person will try to find the other people who have the same song. There is no talking allowed; instead, everyone must hum his song. Use simple songs that everyone knows.

If you have both boys and girls in attendance, they may not feel comfortable with this game. If not, just draw numbers out of a hat.

Once the groups have come together, make sure that each group is fairly even in size and that each has a tape recorder and tape. The groups should be made up of about four or five people. You will want to have three or more groups to make the competition interesting.

After the groups are established, have them sit down together to hear the rest of the instructions. Have each group think of a group name. Give each group a separate room or area to work so as not to disturb the other groups around them.

Instruct the kids that everyone in the group must participate in the recordings. They will be given a list of things to record, and the first group to complete the recordings will win. Stress to the kids that they must record everything on their list or they will not win. I have included a list of suggestions for the recordings at the end of this chapter.

3. Talk and eat

As the groups finish up, ask them to give their cassette tapes of their productions to you, and then let them get a plateful of food while they wait for the other groups to finish. Let everyone eat and talk. They will probably have some funny stories to tell about their group efforts.

4. Listen

As you see people finishing their food, tell them to get their desserts and find a seat in the den to listen to the recordings. Encourage the kids to sit with the other members of their group. Play each tape for the kids. You may want to play back any especially funny parts. Give out simple prizes like a pack of gum or candy to the winners, or you may want to spend a little more money to give small gift certificates to a Christian bookstore.

Now it's time to begin a discussion about the things that kids allow themselves to hear. Show the group the poster cut in the shape of headphones with the theme verse from Mark 4:24, "Take heed what you hear." Start out with the question "What sorts of things do you listen to each day?" They may mention music, movies, teachers, parents, and friends as some of their answers. After several answers have been given, ask the group why they need to be careful.

"What kind of effect do the things you listen to have on you? Does the music you listen to have an impact on your attitude or life? What about movies, or friends, or teachers?"

The conclusion you want the kids to come to is that whatever we put into our minds stays there and many times comes out through our actions and words. Read to the group a few lines from a currently popular secular song. This will help them see more clearly the junk they may be putting into their minds.

Next, read the lyrics to a popular Christian song. Point out the positive effect a song like this will have on their actions in life. Challenge everyone to be careful what they listen to, whether from the radio or from people's mouths. Encourage the kids to ask themselves, *Does this glorify God?* and *Will I be a better person after listening to this?*

If you have time at the end you may want to have some more fun with the tape recorder. Here are some ideas:

Individually record different guests, describing themselves without saying who they are. Play the tape back to the whole group and let them guess who it is.

Pretend that a major disaster has just occurred. Turn the tape recorder on in the middle of the room and record the dramatic scene. You could say it is an earthquake, a tornado, a blizzard, or a tidal wave. Let everyone ham it up and then play it back.

During the party, tell the kids that anyone who wants to tell a joke or scary story should record it on the recorder in the other room. At the end of the party, let the group listen to the recording. You may want to listen and edit first.

Record group emotions. Record the entire group as they laugh hysterically, weep bitterly, scream, giggle, grumble, and so on.

FOOD:

If you have a smaller group and want to serve dinner to your guests, I suggest hamburgers on the grill or buckets of fried chicken. It's simple and just what the kids love! You will want to have plenty of soft drinks since you will be serving them at the beginning of the party and at dinner.

Hamburger or fried chicken
Baked beans
Fruit salad
Chips
Soft drinks
Brownies or giant chocolate chip and oatmeal cookies

If you have a larger group and do not intend to serve a complete meal, I suggest the following snacks:

Bite-size pizzas
Party mix or trail mix
Fruit tray—Offer strawberries, grapes, and apple slices. (Pour lemon or orange juice over the slices to keep them from browning.)
Potato chips and onion dip
Brownies or giant chocolate chip or oatmeal cookies
Soft drinks

FAVORS:

1. Music tape by a Christian artist—Find some on sale or get a quantity discount.
2. Pocket radios—Look for these if you have a small group.
3. Earmuffs, earplugs, or earphones
4. Five-inch mini trash cans—Write on the sides *Garbage in, garbage out* and *Be careful what you listen to.*

List of Recordings

1. Say the alphabet backwards.
2. Quote a phrase or sentence in a foreign language.
3. Repeat something you memorized at school.
4. Make the sound of an egg breaking.
5. Giggle.
6. Laugh hilariously.
7. Say a tongue twister three times fast.
8. Quote a Bible verse that begins with the letter *L*.
9. Bark the song "Row, Row, Row Your Boat."
10. Make the sound of leaves rustling in the wind.
11. Create and perform a rap song about joy.
12. Recite the ten commandments as best you can without looking them up.
13. Sing "The Star Spangled Banner."
14. Make the sound of someone eating an apple.
15. Give a sad cry.
16. Create and recite a poem about peace.
17. List ten things that are blue.
18. Everyone at the same time make barnyard animal sounds.
19. Give a weather report for today.
20. Create and record a commercial for this tape recorder.
21. Sing "Happy Birthday" to the birthday boy or girl.

* 29 *

The Original Pizza Party

Create the most incredible pizza in the world at this event! The kids will prepare the ingredients, then split into teams and make original creations with their pizzas. They will play great group games while the pizzas are cooking, then chow down on the edible creations. Dessert and a discussion about our Creator from Genesis 1:1 will follow.

➡ **Suggested Size:** 6 to 15 kids
Suggested Time of Day: noon or evening
Type: boys, girls, or both

YOU WILL NEED:

- Poster boards
- Construction paper
- Pizza ingredients
- Pizza pans or cookie sheets

- Dessert

INVITATIONS:

Your invitations will look like a slice of pizza with the information written on the back. From white poster board, cut out pizza slices about 8 inches long and 4 inches wide at the top of the slice. Glue red construction paper on the slice to look like tomato sauce. Cut brown shapes to look like mushrooms or sausage and green for peppers and olives. Shred some yellow paper to look like cheese on top. On the back of the slice of pizza write the information for the party as follows:

Create the Most Original Pizza!

Meet at _____ (address)

_____ (date, time)

_____ (number)

RSVP: _____

DECORATIONS:

You may want to make a giant pizza similar to the invitations to use as a welcome sign on the door. Another idea for a welcome sign is to use a large pizza box from a local pizza vendor. Write *Home of World Famous Pizza* and hang it on the door. Use red-checked tablecloths and napkins for the tables. In the center of the tables place baskets or vases with bread sticks.

SCHEDULE: 2 hours

15 minutes—Arrive and prepare ingredients
25 minutes—Break into groups and create pizzas
20 minutes—Games
25 minutes—Eat, judge pizzas
35 minutes—Dessert and discussion

ACTIVITIES:

1. Arrive and prepare ingredients

Have your son or daughter greet the guests at the door. When they arrive they will come into the kitchen and help prepare toppings for the pizza. Let some of the kids grate cheese; others can chop mushrooms and onions, and others can help you cook the hamburger or sausage. There can be a job for everyone. Provide soft drinks and light munchies at this time.

After most of the guests have arrived and all of the toppings are ready, you will need to divide into teams to create the pizzas. Three or four teams is a good number. You do not want to have too many teams or you will not be able to cook all of the pizzas. A good way to divide into teams is to draw three pizzas on poster boards and slice them before the party. Make each pizza with recognizably different ingredients such as pepperoni or mushroom or green pepper. Put the pizza slices in a bag. Have each guest pull a slice out of the bag and match her slice with the others that have the same topping. After they have found the rest of their pizza or group, allow them to decide on a team name. Make sure that the groups are fairly even.

2. Create pizzas

Each group must decide how they want to decorate their pizza. Encourage the groups to think of a theme or design to create with the toppings. Remind them that this is a contest. When we did this party with a group of girls, they made a doggie face pizza, a globe pizza, and a garden pizza, all using the toppings provided. They were fantastic!

For the pizza crust, I suggest using the recipe below. It will be fun for the kids to work with the dough. An easier route would be to use ready-made pizza crust or a can of dinner biscuits. For the tomato filling, I suggest pizza or spaghetti sauce from a jar.

Biscuit Pizza Crust

1 package active dry yeast
3/4 cup warm water
2 1/2 cups boxed biscuit mix

Soften yeast in warm water. Add biscuit mix and beat vigorously for 2 minutes. Knead dough till smooth (25 strokes). Divide dough in half and spread each on greased baking sheets; crimping the edges. Brush dough with oil. Fill with toppings and bake at 425° for 15 minutes or till crusts are done. Makes two 12-inch pizza crusts.

If you do not have enough oven space to cook the pizzas, ask a neighbor if you can use her oven to cook some of the pizzas.

3. Games

Play several games while you wait for the pizzas to cook. Here are some fun suggestions.

Human machine—Let the kids keep the same teams that they had for the pizza creations. Each group decides on a single machine to portray. The machine can be anything with moving parts such as a washing machine, a blender, a car, or a lawn mower. The object of the game is to use everyone in the group to be the parts of the machine. For example, if the group decides to be a car, then one player is the engine making engine noises. Another player is the steering wheel, and another could be the trunk. After the machine is complete, see how well the parts all work together by making sounds and moving parts. Let the other groups try to guess what they are.

After each group has made and demonstrated their machine, then decide on new machines. Set a time limit of three minutes to decide on a machine and produce the parts. If you have a small number of guests, let everyone work together as one group.

Unique you—Give each guest a file card and pencil and ask him to write a description of himself. The description must point out his unique qualities, experiences, and accomplishments—the things that make him unlike any other person in the group. Focus on personality more than physical appearance. The players should not sign their names.

Collect the file cards and shuffle them. Players form a circle and sit on the floor and the file cards are passed out. One by one players read the cards they are holding. The goal is to try to guess, as quickly as possible, the identity of the unique person described on the card.

Namely you—A similar game played by handing out file cards to all of the guests. Let them write their names backward. Read the backward names to the group and let the players try to guess who the name belongs to as quickly as they can. Next, each player can scramble the letters in her name and write it on another card. Pass the cards out again to the kids and let them try to figure out whose name they have.

Another fun thing to do while the pizza is cooking is to work on a jigsaw puzzle that has a picture of a pizza. I have seen pizza jigsaw puzzles at several toy stores.

4. Tasting time

Set all of the pizzas out on a table so everyone can have a good look at them. Instead of cutting the pizzas into the usual slices, cut the pizzas in squares so there will be enough for everyone to have a taste of each pizza.

You and your spouse will judge the different pizzas. Offer awards for originality, creativity, best tasting, and any other award you want to give. The prizes can be small items purchased at a Christian bookstore, such as bookmarks or pencils. You may even check with a local pizza restaurant and ask if they can give you any discount coupons to hand out as prizes.

5. Dessert and discussion

When most people are finished with their pizza, tell them that they can pick up a dessert and sit down in the den to talk. After they have all gathered in the den, announce the winners of the pizza contest.

Begin your discussion by asking the kids what was the best part of creating their pizza. You may want to ask a few questions if they seem to be reluctant to talk. "Was it thinking up the creation or perhaps putting it together?" Next, ask the kids if they found any of the process difficult. Ask them to imagine how difficult it would have been to make the pizza if they had never seen, tasted, or heard of a pizza before.

Show the kids a poster board with Genesis 1:1 written on it. Read the verse to the group. Then say:

Isn't it incredible to think that God made this world from scratch? He made this world out of nothing. It was an original design. You may have found it challenging to create your pizzas, but God created our incredible world. Some people want to say that the world just happened and that you and I just formed together over a process of millions of years. Just think if you left the ingredients for your pizza sitting around for a long, long period of time; do you think they could eventually form a pizza? Your pizzas could not just happen, they needed a creator. You had to think up a plan to make the pizza and produce it. This world is far more complex than any pizza. We didn't just happen; we had a Creator, and He is God. Let's take a moment right now to thank God for His perfect and incredible creation.

After you have prayed, let everyone mingle for a while as they are leaving.

FOOD:

Your preparation will be easy since the kids will be making the pizzas. As I mentioned earlier, you may want to have some bread sticks on the table for a centerpiece and for munching. Cheese, crackers, fruit, and vegetable slices would make good snacks for the kids to nibble on when they arrive.

Soft drinks—Serve a variety of soft drinks. You will need about three 2-liter bottles for every five kids.

Apple pie with vanilla ice cream

FAVORS:

1. Discount coupons to a local pizza restaurant
2. Globe items—Since you discussed Genesis 1:1 about God creating the world, look for any item that may have a globe on it. I have found key chains, Frisbees, erasers, notebooks, and place mats.
3. Polaroid pictures of the groups with their pizzas—Put them in plastic frames with pizzas painted on the corners.

* 30 *
Puzzle Power!

Are you puzzled about the type of party to have for the kids? How about a puzzle theme? Set up several tables with different jigsaw puzzles or let everyone work on one giant puzzle. Kids will listen to Christian music and munch on snacks while they work. The goal is to have fun and finish. Warning: Puzzles can be addictive, and you may be required to hold this party annually or monthly. The theme verse is Romans 8:28: God makes the puzzle pieces of life work together for the good for those who love Him.

➡ **Suggested Size:** 5 to 20 kids
Suggested Time of Day: afternoon or evening, after dinner
Type: boys, girls, or both (some boys would love a party like this, others may not be as interested in coming unless it is boys and girls together—check with your son)

YOU WILL NEED:

- Poster boards, scissors, markers
- Snacks and soft drinks
- Several 250 or 500 piece puzzles

- Puzzle glue
- Tables
- Christian music tapes

INVITATIONS:

Your invitations will be puzzles cut from colored poster board. Cut 5-inch by 7-inch rectangles out of poster board and write the following information:

IT'S PUZZLE-MANIA!

Don't miss the most amazing puzzle put-together in your lifetime!

Place: _____ (address)

Time: _____

Date: _____

RSVP: _____ (number)

Cut up the rectangles to look like puzzles, making about four or five pieces out of each invitation. Put the pieces into envelopes and mail them to your guests. Make sure each envelope has all of its pieces or you may have some confused invitees.

DECORATIONS:

Your decorations can be very simple. Using three or four colored poster boards, make giant puzzle pieces to hang around the room (cut two pieces from each poster). On one of the puzzle pieces write Romans 8:28. Use one of the puzzle pieces to put on the door as a welcome sign.

SCHEDULE: 2 hours

10 minutes—Arrive and mingle
45 minutes—Work on puzzles, snack
20 minutes—Break and discuss verse
45 minutes—Complete puzzles

ACTIVITIES:

1. Arrive and mingle

Have your son or daughter greet the guests at the door and point out where to get soft drinks. Before the party you should decide if everyone will work on one puzzle together or have several puzzles going at once. If you have more than six guests you should have more than one puzzle. Provide a different puzzle for every five to six guests. To divide the guests evenly and fairly at the puzzles, take five or six puzzle pieces from each puzzle and put them into a bag. As the guests arrive, have them pick a puzzle piece out of the bag. The guest will then need to find the puzzle to which his piece belongs. This will be the puzzle he will work on during the party. Make sure there is a fairly even amount of kids at each puzzle. After each guest has obtained a soft drink and found his puzzle, let him get right to work.

2. Work on puzzles, snack

Work on the puzzles while listening to some popular Christian music. I'm sure your son or daughter can help you decide on a tape. Provide plenty of snacks for the puzzle workers. Encourage everyone to participate. If you see someone just sitting at a table, help that person to get involved by urging him to find the edge pieces or pieces that make up a certain item in the puzzle.

Make this a competition between groups, so that the group to finish first is the winning group. You can make the prizes small puzzles, gift certificates, or trophies.

Buy some puzzle glue (available at most toy or craft stores) to seal the puzzles once they are complete. Sealing puzzles is a good project for the groups if they finish sooner than you expect.

3. Break and discuss verse

Take a break after about 45 minutes to rest from working on the puzzles and to talk. Bring out dessert and ask everyone to come and sit down while they eat. Give a progress report as to which team seems to be getting the closest to completion.

Begin your discussion by taking one puzzle piece and holding it up. Remind the kids that when they arrived, they were given just one puzzle piece like the one you are holding. Explain that it is hard to tell much about the puzzle from just that one piece, but it will fit together with other pieces to make a complete picture. Point out that some of the pieces are jagged, some are funny shaped, and some are smooth.

Tell the kids that our lives are kind of like puzzles.

The different events in our lives are like the pieces to the puzzle; they all work together to make a complete picture. God knows what that complete picture looks like for each of our lives, and we must trust that each event He allows to enter our lives is working together for a purpose—purpose of a complete picture.

Romans 8:28 states, "And we know that all things work together for good to those who love God, to those who are the called according to

His purpose." For those who do love God, He has a great plan and purpose for our lives. He is using each event, each puzzle piece, in our lives to complete a beautiful picture. Some of the pieces may not be so nice or enjoyable, while others just seem so smooth and easy. We must trust that He is at work in our lives. The pieces in your puzzle won't fit into someone else's puzzle. Each of our lives is unique and is created for a unique purpose. Let's be thankful for the work He is doing in our lives.

You may want to add some examples of puzzle pieces in our lives or ask the kids to think of some examples. Their answers may be as simple as not getting an *A* on a test, or as difficult as a friend moving away or a relative dying. Point out that puzzle pieces can also be positive events in our lives such as making cheerleader or gaining a new friend. Remind the kids that God uses all of these events to make us into the person He wants us to be.

4. Complete puzzles

Go back to the puzzles and finish. Let those who finish early glue theirs together or help other groups finish. Take a picture of each group with their finished puzzle.

Here are some puzzling games to play if you have some extra time or just want to take a break from the puzzles.

Giant chair—Tell everyone to form a circle, shoulder to shoulder, then turn to her left. When you give the signal, have the players sit down on the lap of the person behind them. They can hold on to the person in front of them if they need to. Now that they are in a sitting position, tell them to each lift their left foot and hold it out. Try different stunts and see how long you can keep the chair intact. This game is best played with all girls or all boys.

Homemade puzzles—Break into teams according to puzzle groups and give each team a piece of construction paper, a pen, and scissors. Each group is to look up a Bible verse or make up a brief story and write it on the paper. Then they should cut it like a puzzle with no more than fifteen pieces. Each team passes their homemade puzzle to the next group. When you give the signal, the teams are to race to put the puzzles together. The team that puts their puzzle together first wins. Each team reads their puzzle out loud to the group.

Brain benders—Give the group fun but challenging problems to solve. Let them solve them as teams or as individuals. You may want to give prizes for those who solve the problems first. Here are some brain benders to try:

- Perplexing Poem

    The beginning of eternity,
    The end of time and space,
    The beginning of every end,
    The end of every place.

- What is being described?
  (Answer: The letter *E*.)

- The following number is the only one of its kind. Can you figure out what is so special about it?

    8,549,176,320

  (Answer: It is the only number that contains all of the numerals in alphabetical order. Eight, five, four, nine, one, and so on.)

- What is weightless, can be seen with the naked eye, and if put in a barrel, will make the barrel weigh less?
  (Answer: A hole.)

- Insert the symbols + and − in the equation below so that it is correct:

    $$2\ 9\ 3\ 5\ 7\ 1 = 9$$

    (Answer: $2 + 9 - 3 - 5 + 7 - 1 = 9$.)

You can find more brain benders from game books in the library or from the school math teacher.

FOOD:

Finger foods and munchies will be the main refreshments for this party. You want to make sure that the food is not messy since kids will be eating while they work.

Soft drinks—You will need approximately three 2-liter bottles for every five kids. Since you are just having munchies, kids tend to drink more soft drinks. It is always better to have leftover drinks than not enough.

Popcorn

Trail mix

Pretzels

Potato chips

Corn chips

Cake—Cut a large sheet cake into puzzle pieces. You can do the same with brownies or a dessert bar.

FAVORS:

1. Miniature jigsaw puzzles—These have become quite popular. You can purchase them at toy stores and party stores for very little.
2. Pocket size challenge games
3. Caps, cups, or T-shirts with the words of Romans 8:28 painted on them.

Closing

I wish you the best as you endeavor to create lasting memories for your family. Here are a few final tips as we close.

1) Do not expect perfection. Just like weddings, children's parties can have small, unexpected glitches. Roll with the punches. Hang loose. When kids are together, they are going to have fun whether the cake flops, the decorations fall or the favors are forgotten. I recently gave a WILD AND WACKY WATER PARTY for my daughter. It rained on the original date and on the rain date. I decided to go ahead with the party and bring it indoors. The kids made bath foam sculptures as they sat on mats on the kitchen floor. They played balloon volleyball using the decorative fish net as a volleyball net. I told the story of Jesus calming the water and then we ate cake, picnic-style in the kitchen. It wasn't my original plan, but the kids had a fantastic time and that's all that matters. Remember that your goal is to provide a fun and memorable experience for the kids.

2) Your farewell is just as important as your greeting. Give a hug and a smile to each guest as they leave. Encourage your child to thank each guest at the door.

3) Let your light shine. Remember that these are not ordinary parties. They are extraordinary because they teach wonderful biblical values. Your example of kindness and love will reaffirm the lesson taught through the party. Let His love shine through you as you welcome these precious little ones into your home.

4) Pray with your family before the party. Pray that the words that you say will have a lasting impact on the lives of your guests. God says in Isaiah 55:11 that His word will not return void. Claim this promise as you prepare to give your party.

My prayer is that God will use these parties for His glory. Have a fantastically fun time and may God bless your efforts.

Carnival, Decoration, and Party Catalog
U.S. Toy Co., Inc.
1227 E. 119th St.
Grandview, MO 64030
1-800-255-6124

Some of the ideas in this book were adapted from:

Bob Gregson, *The Incredible Indoor Games Book* (Belmont, CA: David S. Lake Publishers) 1982.

Karol Ladd graduated from Baylor University in 1982 with a B.S. degree in Education. Formally a teacher, Karol presently works at home as a wife and mother. She has been honored as an Outstanding Young Woman of America, Notable Young Woman of Texas, and co-president of Young Christian Mothers. She is actively involved in her church and community activities. Karol has led several women's Bible study groups as well as several children's Bible story clubs. As a speaker, Karol's creative concepts and lively personality blend together to enlighten and inform her audience.